MANAGEMENT RESPONSES TO EXPENDITURE CUTS

To my family

Management Responses to Expenditure Cuts

PHILIP FRAME
Middlesex Business School
Middlesex Polytechnic

Avebury

Aldershot · Brookfield USA · Hong Kong · Singapore · Sydney

Published by

Avebury

Academic Publishing Group,
Gower House, Croft Road, Aldershot,
Hants GU11 3HR, England

Gower Publishing Company,
Old Post Road, Brookfield, Vermont 05036
USA

A CIP catalogue record for this book
is available from the British Library.

ISBN 1 85628 089 6

Printed and Bound in Great Britain by
Athenaeum Press Ltd., Newcastle upon Tyne.

Contents

Acknowledgments

I would like to thank Drs H. S. Gill and J. McAuley for their support, together with the members of the organisation who provided me with data; and finally Middlesex Business School and Iain McLean for helping me produce the finished version.

1 Introduction

How and why distinct groups of managers in the same organisation responded differently to the instruction to manage a reduction in expenditure is the principal problem explored in this work. A secondary issue, the nature of management sub-cultures, is addressed and utilised in analyzing members' constructions of, and responses to, reduced resources. The researcher used an action research model. The data base for this work is members' accounts. These were analyzed in the light of organisational documents, researcher observation, and relevant academic work.

This introductory chapter examines the genesis of expenditure reductions, sub-cultures and action research, and the issues raised by these topics. It then describes how the issues are presented, and what contribution the work makes to the general stock of knowledge.

Origins of the Research

I became interested in the management of expenditure reductions (defined as an externally enforced reduction of spending) for four reasons: the extensive media coverage of financial reductions at the time the research began; the identification of reductions as a major problem area for members of the organisation who granted access; my personal work experience; and the limited academic attention the subject had received at that time. There is now, however, a growing North American literature.

Over the last decade, from the end of 1979 onwards, there have been numerous media reports on the implementation of financial stringency measures in the public sector. These frequently focussed on the cause (usually defined as resulting from Government policy); on the affected individuals, (both employees and clients); or on conflicts between parties with opposing views. Whilst the coverage was necessarily limited, it left an impression that whereas the management of financial reductions was a novel task for public sector managers, experience of this task was becoming widespread. By implication, reductions were being managed: some form of decision making and implementation process was being adopted. How this new management task was in practice carried out seemed a significant area of study.

An action model of research was adopted for reasons which are explained below. Topics suggested by members of the organisation to be studied were treated as significant. In my initial discussions with managers of the Social Services Department where data was collected, expenditure reduction and its management were identified as being current and problematic issues. This was an area where use could be made of the services I was offering. Although at that initial stage no details emerged of why expenditure reductions were problematic the flavour was conveyed by the use of terms such as 'difficult', 'explosive' and 'sensitive'. It was clear that such reductions were a significant issue for managers.

On the assumption that expenditure reductions could create a high degree of uncertainty, I anticipated a certain amount of affinity with members of the Social Services Department resulting from my own experience of coping with uncertainty at work. During the final two years of the Race Relations Board, members faced an uncertain future. Whilst the organisation was certain to cease existing as a separate unit, what the

2

outcomes of this would be for staff in terms of redundancies, relocations and new types of work, remained unclear. I questioned whether various mechanisms for coping with uncertainty, including withdrawal of labour to force decisions from planners, would be found in another organisation.

The management of expenditure reductions is an area in which interest is now growing, though until recently it commanded little attention amongst organisational theorists. Thus in 1978, Levine felt able to assert that there was an assumption of growth in most organisational literature. This orientation was reflected in the M.Sc. in Organisational Development I undertook prior to beginning this research. Development was defined only in terms of growth; other forms of change, and in particular those associated with resource decline, were not addressed. Resource pressure, though, was not as strong a feature of the environment as it subsequently became. By 1985 however, Murray and Jick acknowledged a 'remarkably large body of literature' (p. 112) in the area.

Despite this growing body of literature, which comes mainly from North America, there is as yet no indepth study or ethnography of how managers respond to instructions to reduce expenditure, and why they respond in the ways they do. Glennester (1980) suggests that

> more evidence of organisational practice is needed before we can test these hypotheses further. It is important to study closely and at close quarters just how authority members, officials and professionals are reacting to different sources of constraint, (p. 381).

This work provides evidence of practice in respect of one of these groups, which Glennester terms 'officials'; here it is described as 'managers'.

My interest in this subject grew, then, from my own experience as a recipient of information from the media, and as an employee. Organisation practice and academic texts confirmed that it was an area of work with practical and theoretical value.

Focus of the Research

The research focusses primarily on such questions as why expenditure reductions management was problematic and whether all managers perceived reductions as difficult. In practice, this involved discovering how and why managers responded to the instruction to cut expenditure and whether such an instruction had any effect on the way management carried out its job. How far, it was speculated, did managers redefine their roles in response to such instructions?

Many writers assume that managers are 'economic men' (Martin and Fryer: 1970) who act primarily in terms of formal rationality on the issue of expenditure reductions. On the contrary, authors such as Weber (1968), Eldridge (1968) and Glennester (1980) offer evidence of the variety of rationalities in use in an organisation. An economic view of the manager may well limit a comprehensive exploration of the issues associated with reductions by assuming that problems will be financial rather than behavioural. Whilst the financial aspect is not insignificant, the process of managing expenditure reductions was identified as equally important. This process included a variety of responses and rationalities.

In the literature on expenditure reductions, the assumption of 'economic man' manifests itself in a particular form which I term 'organisational monetarism'. This concept suggests efficiency or rationality gains from resource loss. It is used by authors such as Bogue (1972), McTighe (1979), Stewart (1980), and Davies and Morgan (1981), although they do not use the term 'organisational monetarism'. Does this concept clarify the experiences of organisational managers and is some form of organisational slack beneficial (Cyert and March: 1963) or unhealthy? Does less 'money' in practice result in defensive concentration of managers' energies towards self and group preservation, and to the detriment of flexibility and forward planning, notions of effectiveness and efficiency, and change of any sort?

The failure to address the variety of managerial responses to adversity stems from the adoption of a unitary view both by managers who are termed 'senior', and by writers on organisations. For example, Staw et al (1981) points out that

> current models emphasise organisational, and not individual or group, responses to adversity (p. 501).

4

In this work the extent to which senior managers' views are similar to those of middle managers is examined, and the variety of views and actions is exposed. By focusing on groups this research expands and qualifies the work of Staw et al. The problem of expenditure reductions is the effective management of resources; it is also the ineffective management of variety.

A concern with exploring the variety of management responses to expenditure reductions was facilitated by an analysis of the nature of organisational sub-cultures, and in particular those associated with management teams. Access negotiations changed the focus of the research away from sub-cultures and towards expenditure reductions as the major topic.

An interest in organisational sub-cultures predated contact with the Social Services Department, and was the research focus of the agenda for negotiating access. In the initial approach to the Department, I identified organisational sub-cultures, and the interaction between different group cultures, as a research area of interest. The access agenda included an expressed willingness to examine a mutually agreed topic identified by organisational members. The topic so identified was the management of expenditure reductions. The agreed research agenda involved then both sub-cultures and expenditure reductions with the emphasis on the latter. In fact, it was in the context of expenditure reductions, and the effects of this on intergroup relations between management teams, that an interest in group sub-cultures was expressed by organisational managers. This interest was confirmed during the process of data collection, as was the growing significance to managers of expenditure reductions.

In adopting an action model, which involved both advancing theory and helping clients, a client-identified problem area was desirable as a starting point. The research was thus both client-centred and researcher-centred, and involved a degree of flexibility in terms of topic selection. One advantage of this approach is that members may be more, rather than less, willing to 'own' the resultant data and its analysis, because they have been involved in the selection of the problem to be researched. Client action, it is argued, is then more likely.

Access can be difficult to obtain to study issues which organisational members find sensitive or threatening. An approach based on a stated focus of expenditure reductions may have led to rejection, because of the anxiety this topic created. This assumption was confirmed when a direct but

5

unsuccessful approach (described in Chapter 2), was made to another organisation. In contrast, sub-cultural phenomena was a non-threatening topic for obtaining access.

Organisational Sub-Cultures

In my work experience the focus of investigations of racially discriminatory acts was organisationally specific practice, and the logic or rationality in use. In obtaining members' accounts of particular rules and regulations, and custom and practice, I became aware of the variety of practice amongst organisations in respect of, for example, promotion procedures. At the same time, discovering the reasons behind particular actions involved questioning the rationale involved, the 'taken for granted' assumptions (Schutz: 1973; Schein: 1985) of decision makers, about the qualities and characteristics of ethnic minorities.

When, as Training Officer for the Race Relations Board, I monitored the progress of new employees, I was made aware of the 'taken for granted' nature of much work activity, and the differences between organisations. For example those with experience of other organisations made 'mistakes', that is, they applied a task definition which was appropriate to their previous workplace rather than their current one. The 'taken for granted' nature of such definitions was thereby exposed, and mistakes were dealt with by explicitly defining the expectations members had of the neophyte in relation to the task in question.

Thus at both a common sense and a professional level I was aware of differences in organisational practice, and the 'taken for granted' nature of much of this practice.

My undergraduate training in social anthropology - the observation and analysis of social interaction - gave me a perspective on social activity which recognised the existence of different groupings within the whole. It led me to ascribe prime legitimacy to the accounts of group members, or 'emic' descriptions, as the basis for analysis. It also pointed me in the methodological direction of collecting data by participating as an observer within groups being studied.

During data collection for my M.Sc. dissertation (Frame: 1979) differences between the three divisions of a government funded research institution - pure research, applied research and administration - were highlighted by members. The dimensions identified then were: orientation towards management and the environment (Lorsch and Lawrence: 1965); technology and territory (Miller: 1959); environmental constituents and rate of change (Duncan: 1972); level of environmental uncertainty (Perrow: 1967) and significant others (Shibutani: 1971).

In literature on organisations, culture is a topic which has received some attention from, for example, Jacques (1951), Handy (1978), Pettigrew (1979), and Schein (1985), usually in the form of one organisation having one culture Cultural plurality within an organisation, or the existence of organisational sub-cultures, is referred to, though infrequently explored, by authors such as Bennis (1969) and Handy (1976). Silverzweig and Allen (1976) state that

> every sub-group within each business organisation has its own distinctive set of norms or cultural influences (p. 33).

As an analytical device, group culture is sometimes considered to provide only a partial explanation of intergroup difficulties (Burns and Stalker: 1966).

In a comprehensive survey of the literature on organisational culture Schein (1985) asserts that

> an organisation tends to be a conglomeration of sub-cultures (p. 43).

He does not, through, explore this issue in any detail. It is, he suggests, an empirical question, best answered by researching particular organisational settings. Schein's data tends to support a unitary view of organisational culture, with one exception. He notes the occurrence of sub-cultures in the mid-life of organisations, that is, when the founder and his family are no longer in a dominant position. In part, this work focusses on management sub-cultures, and thus builds on and expands the work of Schein.

In literature on expenditure reductions, culture is infrequently addressed, though a number of authors (Hirschhorn and Associates: 1983) refer to culture as a significant but inhibiting factor in organisational change aimed at facilitating reductions. Their terms 'professional culture' and 'management culture' remain largely undefined. The significance of a cultural approach to scarcity at the macro level is emphasised by Stanley (1968); scarcity must

> first be defined culturally in terms of the available systems
> of meaning (p. 866).

A cultural approach, which attaches significance to an organisation's 'meaning-making' systems is also identified by Nottenburg and Fedor (1983). The cultural form which they term myth influences an organisation's response to decline because it has

> the role of providing meaning for past events and
> constraining the alternatives for future action (p. 334)

Sub-cultures may be differentiated from more transitory phenomena which influence managerial action, such as fashion or a 'flavour of the month' approach, in that sub-cultures exist and persist over time, and so provide a means of evaluating and introducing new developments. At the same time, of course, sub-cultures change; they grow, develop and decline; they are not fixed for all time and any analysis needs to be aware of their changing nature.

A particularly significant source of group sub-culture is derived from professional training. Such training provides the individual with a normative model for carrying out professional duties. When the professional becomes a manager this model is utilised in the performance of the managerial role. Those who have experienced similar training will subscribe to similar values, and it is these that will form the basis of the group sub-culture. It is predicted that, irrespective of the particular organisational setting, groups with similar training will subscribe to and be guided in their management by similar sub-cultural norms. Changes in the course of the professionalisation process will directly influence the form and content of a particular sub-culture.

Methodological Focus

Methodologically the cultural perspective defined by Stanley (1968) as members' views seemed appropriate as a starting point. Analytically, I wanted to know whether cultural traits invariably inhibited reduction-related change. I also wished to explore the nature of the interaction between a group's sub-culture and expenditure reduction events, and the extent to which a cultural explanation is limited.

As a basis for this I firstly considered whether management team cultures existed, how they were maintained and elaborated, and their content and function. Following Schein (1985) my definition of culture emphasises the 'taken for granted', or unquestioned, nature of these phenomena in organisation life. Culture includes ways of thinking, working and evaluating: the term comprehends the conceptual, behavioural and evaluative aspects of action. The term sub-cultures is used to designate the culture peculiar to particular organisational groupings, in this case, management teams.

My definition of the term 'action research' follows Rapoport (1970):

> Action research aims to contribute both to the practical concerns of people in an immediate problematic situation, and to the goals of social science by joint collaboration within a mutually acceptable ethical framework (p. 499).

He suggests it is the immediacy of the researcher' involvement in the action process which distinguishes it from other forms of applied research. My commitment to this approach grew, in part, from the theoretical inputs to the M.Sc. in Organisational Development where it was the preferred mode for initiating organisational change. It seemed an appropriate way of simultaneously advancing theory and addressing practical managerial problems leading to an involvement in organisational change. Particularly this seemed appropriate as prior to the course referred to above, I had been recommending organisational changes in, for example, promotion procedures for ethnic minorities.

I was keen to do a piece of applied research which had relevance to, and was based on, an involvement in organisational practice and which simultaneously made a theoretical contribution. In particular, I wanted to produce something which was of value to, and would be used by, any organisation which provided me with data. Pragmatically, such an approach was said to facilitate access though I found in practice that this was not invariably the case. In addition to putting action research into practice, I wished to improve my skills in consulting: obtaining access, and negotiating and implementing solutions. How an intervention was utilised by members would also be a useful source of information to test the researcher' diagnosis.

In this work three aspects of the action research process are addressed: the problem of access; an action intervention as a diagnostic tool; and action in circumstances of overt conflict.

Structure

The book comprises eight further chapters. The purpose of Chapter 2 is twofold: firstly to set out the methodology used and secondly to discuss organisational access. The first part of the chapter justifies the epistemological perspective and the methodology of data collection and analysis.

In the second part of Chapter 2, the problem of access is addressed both generally and with specific reference to organisations experiencing expenditure reductions. Access and how it is achieved is a significant issue, yet action researchers' reports often take for granted this aspect of their work, usually because they were invited in by the client system. Accounts of field researchers are analysed, to determine those sources of influence which facilitate self initiated access. Access is addressed at an early stage in this study, not only because it took place at the beginning of the research work, but also because it was useful in preliminary organisational diagnosis.

Chapter 3 provides the theoretical context within which the data in subsequent chapters is considered. This scene setting is most logically placed towards the beginning of this account. Firstly the literature on expenditure reductions is reviewed and the concept of organisational monetarism is identified and elaborated to locate the research within the development of academic work in this field.

Data on the precipitating events is also presented in Chapter 3. The instructions to reduce expenditure, and the terminology in use by members to define them is described. A knowledge of how expenditure reductions were introduced will assist understanding of material presented in subsequent chapters. A consideration of terminology as a means of defining the reality of reductions provides an introduction to the variety of meanings placed on the subject by organisational managers.

Chapter 4 contains a consideration of management sub-cultures: whether they are perceived by members, how they are maintained and elaborated, and their content and function. Though this is not the primary focus of the research, it remains a topic of major significance to the analysis of expenditure reductions management. Chapter 4 provides a basis for exposing and analysing the impact of culture on decline management, and thus our understanding of managerial responses in this task area, by introducing the notion of management group sub-cultures. It identifies and elaborates the meaning and content of sub-cultures for both organisational managers and the researcher. Data in subsequent chapters support the view that a group's sub-cultures strongly influences collective responses to stringency, and that stringency in turn influences the sub-cultures of a group.

Expenditure reductions pressure is treated as an example of what Pettigrew (1979), (following Turner: 1957), terms a 'critical event': that is, one which exposes a group's culture to an extent not usually apparent in routine activities. In critical events, debate around appropriate action takes place, and 'taken for granted' assumptions are exposed. In practice, the extent to which reductions were interpreted as a threat over time, or the facility with which they were routinised, exposes the relationship between a group's sub-cultures and the management of expenditure reductions.

In addition a sub-cultural perspective is significant in analysing stringency for the following reasons. Group related values and behaviours were a popular explanatory device used by social service managers to account for responses to financial decline. A focus on sub-cultures facilitated the analysis of variety in behaviour and values observed by both members and the researcher, in respect of different management groups. Thus 'management' was not treated uniformly and there was no assumption of unanimity. At the same time, a sub-cultural focus enabled the significance of behavioural issues, as well as financial issues, to be considered: that is, the analysis of expenditure reductions was not confined solely to a consideration of financial management. A focus on sub-cultures enabled the assertion that culture invariably inhibits reduction-related organisational change

11

(Hirschhorn and Associates: 1983) to be critically examined and more specifically stated in terms of which cultural traits inhibit reductions management and which do not.

Chapter 5 examines the way managers responded to an instruction to reduce expenditure. An account is provided of the variety of strategies adopted, and the justification for these strategies.

Members' categories for strategies - 'resisting' and 'cooperating' - are identified and three defensive reactions, including resistance, are elaborated and examined by reference to the literature. The type of responses predicted by organisational monetarism were found to be absent in practice.

Chapter 6 utilises the content of the two previous chapters to analyse managers' interpretations of their role in expenditure reductions using members' own descriptive terms. Interpretations varied in that, for example, managers who formed the team which subscribed to values such as consultation and democratic management were much less certain that their actions, which were classified as resistance, were appropriate. In addition this chapter contains a report of the changes to intragroup and intergroup relations, none of which accord with the predictions of organisational monetarism.

The action intervention, which included the organisation's two middle management teams and focused on intergroup relations and expenditure reductions, is described and analysed in Chapter 7. The advisability of action in circumstances of overt conflict is considered together with the source of conflict. The intervention produced data which was particularly important to the analysis because it served to emphasise and direct attention to the contextual features as well as to the values, which managers reported as influencing their ability to act. It determined the difference between 'being able to' and 'wanting to' manage reductions.

In Chapter 8 factors which facilitate and inhibit reductions management are addressed by comparing the organisation's two middle management teams, and critically examining some assumptions on which the concept of organisational monetarism is based. Sub-cultural and contextual features are identified as either helping or hindering reductions management, thus continuing the analysis from the previous chapter. In addition, members' views of the future are examined, to determine whether the positive innovations predicted by organisational monetarism were anticipated. In fact members' perceptions of the future were invariably negative.

Chapter 9 summarises the contribution of this research to knowledge in the areas addressed. It defines the limitations of the work and areas for future research. The major contribution is to the theory of managing expenditure reductions, and the influence of both management sub-cultures and contextual features. It meets the need identified by Glennester (1980) for more evidence of organisational practice (p. 381) in order to advance theory. At a descriptive level, the work presents a detailed picture of how management in one organisation responded to the instruction to reduce expenditure, and the variety of management tasks involved. The analysis shows that management groups construct the meaning of expenditure reductions in different ways, and thus respond diversely to the instruction to reduce resources. These constructions seem to owe more to the nature of the context within which groups work, and their respective sub-cultures, than to any behavioural imperative inherent in reduced circumstances. What seems significant is the extent of congruence between context/sub-cultures and the required expenditure reductions. Where there is congruence, managing reductions is relatively straightforward. Where there is less congruence, management is problematic. To deal with reductions then, managers need to 'be able to' as well as 'want to'.

Data on management practice is provided which enhances the value of both the predictive and prescriptive literature, enabling both theoretical constructs and practical advice to be tested against the realities of managing expenditure reductions.

Financial stringency, and therefore the management of stringency, continues to be an issue for the public and the private sectors. The issues which are explored in this work continue to have contemporary relevance both for the practising manager and for the organisational theorist. Decline management remains a relatively under-explored area, particularly at the micro-organisational level.

Conclusion

In concluding this introduction, it may be useful to say something of my personal values in relation to the subject of expenditure reductions. As an issue, it is particularly value-laden: it is sensitive, conflict producing, and a current and overt party political issue.

Prior to the research I had an expectation that fewer resources lead to a reduction in service rather than to an improvement in efficiency. Because of the positive value I attached to organisations affected, I regarded managers' active co-operation in implementing reductions as undesirable. Now I am less sure: diametrically opposed and conflicting managerial responses were each seen as having validity by different managers in the same organisation. Ideologically I hold the view that society has a responsibility to provide for those in need, and that reductions which are unrelated to a decrease in demand are unjustifiable. However, how the manager anticipates and deals with fewer resources has for me become more problematic. Managing is no longer seen as undesirable; rather in fact the reverse, because the effects of not managing the resources that remain may be as damaging to service delivery and inter-managerial relations as the effects of the financial reductions themselves. Both resistance and managing, as strategies at the disposal of managers, are discussed later in Chapter 5.

Whilst asserting that value-free sociology is impossible, Becker (1971) suggests that a charge of bias, or accepting the perspective of one organisational group, is less likely where there is overt conflict:

> the right to define the nature of reality becomes a matter for argument .... the researcher is made aware that there are at least two sides to the story (p. 130).

Overt conflict was reported by members, and observed in the organisation studied. Whilst this was problematic for managers, and for the interventionist, it was beneficial to the researcher because at leat two sides to the story were revealed.

In his essay 'On Methodology', Becker (1971) stresses the importance of the researcher making 'imaginative use of personal experience' (p. 22). This introductory chapter indicates how I have used my experience, as an employee, as a student, and as an action researcher, in generating the issues which are considered in this book. What these issues are, and the stages at

14

which they are addressed, are set out. The contributions to knowledge are indicated, and my own value position in relation to the major focus of the research - the management of expenditure reductions - is elaborated.

2 Methodology and access

Introduction

This chapter provides the epistemological and methodological bases for the research, and then addresses the issue of access. The actor's interpretation of events, and resultant behaviour, forms the basis of the analysis. Data, obtained by interview, document search, and observation was used to devise categories of information which were then compared to the literature. Sources of influence in obtaining access are then considered using reports by both field and action researchers. Finally, access in circumstances of resource stringency is examined in the light of empirical data.

Actor's Perspective

Though Schutz (1967) terms the actor `the forgotten man of sociology', a number of writers support the prominence which he gives to the actor's perspective. In his review of the 'action approach' to the study of organisations, Silverman (1970) provides examples of research which focus on the construction and reconstruction of reality by social acts on the part of actor. Schutz (1973) states that if the social sciences aim indeed at explaining social reality, then the scientific constructs on the second level must include a reference to the subjective meaning an action has for the actor (p. 20).

That is, the analysis, or `second level of constructs', is based on the actor's interpretation, or `first level constructs'. The actor is the source of data on what his activities mean to him, and thus to understand these activities we must refer to the actor.

A number of expressions are used to identify this perspective: 'actor's perspective', 'action perspective', and 'first order constructs'. Schutz also refers to 'common-sense understanding' and 'subjective interpretations' as his focus. Similarly, the Weberian term 'Verstehen' refers to the participant's understanding of his situation. Examples of authors who have used this perspective to advantage are Becker (1971), Dalton (1959) and Roy (1955 and 1973).

A further advantage of this focus lies in the richness and variety of perspectives which are produced. Members' own models are particularly important for this study which is, in part, exploratory, in that it concerns a relatively new and under-researched area of managerial activity.

The Nature of Qualitative Data

Because of its methodological focus, work of this nature is less systematic than, for example, experiments or surveys. Variations on the theme of observer participation assume that the best way to obtain members' perspectives is to observe them in practice. Thurley (1971) for example, suggests that

> structured questionnaires are of little value in catching the meaning behind many of the actions of tenants, operatives and foremen (p. 272).

Instead he recommends semi-structured interviews and observation. Yet it has been argued that these methods, which are usually described as qualitative, are less `scientific', because, for example, the observer can mould the data he obtains to fit his own preconceptions. In fact, as Becker (1971) points out, this is less likely than with more systematic methods. The richness of data obtained frequently requires the observer

> to sacrifice his pet ideas and hypotheses to recalcitrant facts
> in his field notes (p. 43).

Another criticism of this method involves the possibility of researcher 'going native', or accepting and adopting members' perspectives to the detriment of his researcher role. This assumes, though, a consistency of perspective within an organisation and amongst its members. This was not apparent in my experience. Whilst accepting members' perspectives as they were presented, the conflicting perspectives obtained made it extremely difficult to regard one set as 'correct'. A measure of objectivity resulted from these very differences. Additionally the research is not confined to a presentation of members' views, but rather uses these as a basis for analysis.

On a pragmatic note, qualitative data is more likely to facilitate the internalisation of information by members and to elicit action. Research by Van der Vall et al (1976) indicates that action is more likely to be taken on qualitative research data than on quantitative data. They define 'quantitative' to include survey research, whilst 'qualitative' refers to participant observation and case study analysis.

Observer Participation

I term my method of data collection observer participation to distinguish it from the more usual term of participant observation. This latter term has been used to describe a range of relationships between the researcher and his data source. Gold's (1958) typology of research methods provides a useful starting point to consider the elements of my relationship with social services managers.

Gold defines four relationships between the researcher and the data sources, using two sets of categories:

(a)   overt and covert: whether or not the researcher's purpose is known to the subjects

(b)   participation and formal observation: whether or not the researcher is involved in social interaction with subjects.

These categories are tabulated as follows:

FIGURE 1

RESEARCH RELATIONS GOLD (1958)

	OVERT	COVERT
PARTICIPATION	*Participation as Observer*	*Covert Participation*
FORMAL OBSERVATION	*Observer as Participant*	*Covert Formal Observation*

My activities were 'overt', and involved both participating as an observer, and observing as a participant. With the former, according to Gold, both parties know the relationship is one for field-research purposes, but the researcher participates in group activities. Being an observer as participant on the other hand entails one-visit interviews and formal observations. In general, my method alternated between these two.

Further examination of my own experience led me to question the extent to which it is possible to categorise research activities into participating or observing. Rather than regarding these as either/or categories it would be more useful to regard them as lying at either end of a continuum, with the researcher moving back and forth, depending on his requirements and the exigencies of the field.

In addition to the above categories, Gold also refers to informal and formal, though it is unclear whether he is referring to the activities of members or researcher. Assuming this applies to both, and combined with the categories identified in Figure 1, the following model can be drawn up.

FIGURE 2
DIMENSIONS OF RESEARCHER ACTIVITY AND FOCUS

1 Researcher Activity	*participation......* *observation*
2 Research Method	*formal......informal*
3 Researcher's Purpose	*covert......overt*
4 Members' Activity	*formal......informal*

The first dimension distinguishes between the researcher's active participation in members' activities, and passive data collection by observation. Formal and informal methodologies define the extent to which data collection procedures are structured, specified and restricted prior to the data-producing event. The third dimension identifies the extent of members' knowledge of the researcher's purpose. The fourth and final dimension distinguishes between members' activities resulting from the occupation of a particular position within the organisation, and the less structured social interactions between members as they carry out their formally defined tasks.

The first three dimensions represent the 'how' of the research process, or its operationalisation, and the last one represents the 'what' or the focus of research activities. Using these, the researcher's activities can be described more adequately. In fact, the researcher's relationship is in a fluid state, and will move backward and forward between the extremes represented by the above continuum. An example will illustrate this point.

As I was in the organisation on a daily basis for a number of months, I was able to observe and talk to members informally and thus participate in the social life of the organisation. Additionally I participated as a member when obtaining stationery, and trivial changes here provided me with an example of the effect of expenditure reductions. Control was imposed by requiring completion of a `request for stationery' form, and the obtaining of a superior's signature whereas previously a verbal request had been sufficient.

My activities were not confined to Gold's definition of an `observer as participant' yet I did not perform the activities associated with the role of manager. For example, when I observed meetings I did not contribute to the discussion or raise items for consideration though I did participate at an informal, process level. I chatted with other members before and during breaks and after meetings. I passed out tea and biscuits and collected money for these, much as any other member would do. I was always a part of the group being observed, either sitting round a table or in a circle, rather than sitting outside it. I participated in general responses, such as laughing at jokes, and acknowledging eye contact, smirks or looks of impatience. Thus in Gold's terms I was a `participant as observer'.

In fact during the course of one meeting I could be involved sequentially in participating in informal activities, and observing informal or formal activities: pre-meeting chat; observation; passing round papers; observation; passing round tea; observation; post-meeting talk. Latterly I was also involved as an active participant in the action intervention I initiated for and with members. Thus the researcher's role is more usefully characterised as being in a fluid state, moving along the four dimensions referred to above.

I now examine my three methods of data collection in some detail, namely interviewing, observation and documentary analysis.

Data Collection

1) Interviewing

I saw members individually to obtain information by a process of question and answer. General questions areas were determined prior to the interview, but the process was sufficiently flexible to allow other matters to be probed. I was interested in the individual's job; accounts of contact with and impressions of other divisions; involvement in expenditure reductions; and the individual's responses to expenditure reductions with their reasons. The questions I asked were usually open ended to allow members to select for themselves the data they gave, and to reduce the likelihood of my influencing what data was offered. For example, I would ask 'what about the cuts?' or 'did the cuts affect you?' or 'were you involved in the cuts?' Of course more specific questions demanding particular pieces of information were asked to clarify detailed points.

As I was interested in managers' perspectives, I interviewed all management members of the organisation, usually on two occasions, and observed them in operation in their three respective management teams: Directors management team (D.M.T.), Field Work management team (F.W.M.T.), and Residential and Day Care management team (R. and D.C.M.T.).

Interviews serve to provide the individual's perspective on the issues being considered, and to expand and re-orientate information and impressions obtained from other sources, including other interviews. It enables the researcher to check on what has or has not been said at meetings, and to discover how far the individual's position varied from that of other group members. The informant is aware that the researcher will see him in other settings and will therefore be less inclined to present an image which varies too much from his usual public one.

2) Observation

Observation took place in two settings. As a temporary member with office space on the organisation's central site, I observed some of the day-to-day life that went on there. This enabled me to get the feel of the organisation and acquire the knowledge to understand incomplete references to the site in other settings, and to chat to members as I walked around. The other and more significant setting was meetings of the organisation's three management teams. I sat in on a series of meetings of each group and noted what topics were discussed. Of particular interest were references ,to expenditure reductions and comments on out-group members.

As well as providing data on substantive matters, each group's process provided diagnostic material on matters such as how they conducted their meetings. A group's process provided data on the creation and re-creation of that group's culture. It was, therefore, of particular significance in discovering the dimensions of culture, and in determining whether any of these dimensions facilitated or inhibited reduction-related management tasks. Conversely process was also of interest in identifying the extent to which group culture was affected by the advent of the expenditure reductions task. Finally I was able to compare public contributions with those made to me privately, and thus check on the reliability of the latter.

By observing a number of meetings of each group I reduced the possibility of stressing an unrepresentative event. Thus I sat in on six meetings of the organisation's senior management team (D.M.T.). I was able to follow the progress of items which were, or were not dealt with over time, such as the issue of financial control by the Field Work Management Team (F.W.M.T.). As these meetings were at different levels in the organisation, I was able to observe how the same item was dealt with at these different levels. Thus a discussion paper on the management of expenditure reductions for field work managers was initially presented to senior management and then to the F.W.M.T. By observing two teams at the same horizontal level a comparison was made of the issues they considered and of the similarities or differences between the ways they dealt with them. Finally I attended joint meetings between the two middle management teams, in order to observe how they functioned together.

A number of authors are critical of observation as a means of data collection. For example, Blumer (1971), from his symbolic-interactionist perspective, maintains that behaviour in groups can only be usefully understood by participating in the meaning-making activities of the group. Non-participation he suggests, can lead to 'the worst kind of subjectivism' (p. 188), where the 'objective' observer's surmises are substituted for those of the actor's. Schutz (1967) makes a similar point: the meanings assigned by actors and observers to an action may be different. He points out that negative actions, or actions which were considered and rejected, are obviously not apparent to the researcher who has no knowledge of them or of the reasons lying behind such choices. But if the researcher has access to members, he can check his surmises, and their reasons for negative actions. Thus for example I asked Field Work managers why managing expenditure reductions was not raised by them in team meetings since I knew from interviews that it was a management problem.

Criticism of observation is based on a definition of what is observed which is limited to overt physical actions. Meetings were also fora where items were discussed and reasoned out, argued about, or responded to. Sometimes only bald statements were made, for example, 'cuts are against everything we stand for'. Sometimes the grounds for adopting a particular position were justified to other members. Often these discussions represented off-the-cuff responses to the issue. Sometimes they were a repetition of old arguments, and on occasions they were 'planned', that is, members decided before the meeting what they were going to say. Nevertheless, the substance of members' contributions was of interest to the observer for they provided an insight into the group's creation and re-creation of reality.

It has been suggested that an observer influences a group. This is less likely if observation takes place over time, as in this study. Becker (1971) suggests this is because 'putting on a show' becomes difficult to sustain. Members are also 'enmeshed in social relationships which are important to them' (p. 46) which, Becker suggests, are a more potent force than the researcher's influence.

A continuing presence over time also aids the researcher's social interaction with members as individuals. He becomes familiar and thus less threatening. Members know the researcher is in an informed position because of his observations; it provides a joint experience which can be referred to later in individual settings.

3) Documentary Analysis

I examined minutes of the two middle management team meetings for a period prior to, and during my time with the organisation. I was unable to examine minutes of the Director's management team meetings as none were produced. I obtained information on the frequency of meetings, their form, and the issues which had been considered. Any reference to expenditure reductions and to relations with other divisions were of particular interest. In addition I scrutinised discussion papers which were circulated at meetings I attended, paying particular attention to those which concerned expenditure reductions. One of these detailed how their team leader suggested the F.W.M.T. should deal with the effects of expenditure reductions. The other represented a F.W.M.T. strategy for exerting influence on councillors by providing them with information on the effects of reductions in the field work division.

Reservations about the use of written material as a source of data often focus on the disadvantages of retrospection when no one involved either in producing or receiving them is available to interpret their meanings except with hindsight. This criticism often also applies to recent documents in cases where the researcher has no access to the producers and their intended meanings, nor the recipients and their interpretations. But such criticism is less relevant if the researcher has access to producers and recipients, as I did. This is not to argue that documents have only one set of meanings. What is of interest is the intended purpose of such documents and how they are interpreted by the audience for which they were produced. Thus Cicourel (1964) states that historical documents

> may contain idiomatic expressions, group specific jargon or connotations which the researcher must try to determine without prior knowledge of the writer's objectives or ways of interpreting the world (p. 154)

Access to members enables the researcher to overcome this, particularly if he was present at the events which form the substance of these documents, and if he was present at their creation. In fact, the creation process itself was illuminating for often minutes made no reference to lengthy discussions, or contained a much shorter version. Questions such as 'Shall I put that in the minutes?', 'How shall I phrase that?', or 'I don't think we'll include that in the minutes', were signs that an account of the group' performance was being created for the benefit of non-group members. Thus group members were conscious that minutes were a means of influencing non-members and some referred to minutes in this way.

Data Analysis

I examined and compared data as I went along, looking for links and contradictions between what had been obtained from different sources. These links were used to form categories of data. The data was then re-examined in the light of these categories, to check for information which might have been overlooked, or which might have become relevant in the light of the categories devised. An example will serve to illustrate this.

During a number of interviews I was told that there was a lack of interest in the financial control aspect of management in the F.W.M.T. This was linked to the group's response to expenditure reductions. It was also linked with their team leader's statement to me about his intention to introduce a regular review of spending, or 'calendarisation', at this group's meetings. (Calendarisation involved a comparison of actual spending during a month with a notional figure, arrived at by dividing total annual budget, in each spending area, by twelve. Under this system, spending per month should roughly match the month's budget. If it does not, overspending or underspending is identified). From my observation I noted that he did not in fact do this. The difference in practice here between the F.W.M.T. and the R. and D.C.M.T. was pointed out by a number of managers, and I could and did confirm this from observation and from minutes. A difference in practice was apparent between the two middle management teams: R. and D.C.M.T., unlike their F.W. colleagues, did consider current spending on a regular basis as a matter of course. I also observed differences between the two groups in terms of their respective resource allocating skills, their views of these skills, and financial management in general. Thus the category of 'financial management' emerged as a theme around which numerous pieces of data, from interview, observation and documents, could be organised. This organised data was then examined in the light of data from other categories, such as 'responses to reductions' and with literature on organisational decline.

Continuing this example, I concluded that an interest in, and experience of the financial aspect of management, was a significant factor in determining group reactions to the instruction to recommend and manage expenditure reductions and to an organisational climate where an emphasis on financial constraint was seen to be increasing.

In presenting my analysis, transcripts of the spoken and written word are shown as quotations but without a page reference, otherwise a summary of the relevant data is presented. The source of the data is also indicated; usually this is a member of one of the organisation's three management teams. What is quoted represents a 'typical' remark because it was echoed by a significant number of members in one form or another.

My aim in presenting the literature is to integrate it with my data. Traditionally a research report is introduced by a literature review but this may sometimes create a gap between the work of others and the author's own research. Instead an attempt is made at integration by presenting what others have contributed when a particular theme is discussed. This method also symbolises the data-led rather than the literature-led nature of this study. There are, however, a number of points about the literature that do not fit easily into the body of the work. Additionally there is a major theme in the literature - improvements through reductions, or what I term organisational monetarism - which is not suggested by the data. Because it represents an opposite view it is a useful analytical device to examine both the significance of the theme itself and the realities of the Social Services Department. I now consider the process of gaining access as a source of organisational data.

Access

In order to determine what facilitates access to an organisation to collect data, I analysed my own experience as a researcher committed to action research, and accounts by both action and field researchers. Of particular interest was whether the reality of expenditure reductions was a significant factor in determining access. Indeed the degree to which an organization is open to access is important generally in diagnosing the readiness for change of an organisation. The ways members react to the novelty of having an action researcher amongst them give an early indication of readiness or resistance. In order to examine access, it is necessary to identify forms and sources of influence.

The term access is used to define the initial stages of organisational contact when permission to gather data is being negotiated, and to distinguish this process from the first stage of action research which has been termed 'entry' by Gill (1982) or 'scouting and entry' by Gill (1975 b), and Henley (1975). These latter terms relate to activities after official permission for access has been given.

Access is clearly an important issue, for on it depends the future of both field and action research. That it is problematic is recognised by a number of authors. Delaney (1960) for example points to

> the relative inaccessibility of organisations for research purposes (p. 450).

Sofer (1961) refers to

> the problem of access that dogs the empirical sociological study of contemporary society (p. 110).

Strategies to overcome this are elusive. Beck (1970) points out that

> there are no easy formulae to finding your way through such (access) interviews (p. 14).

In view of the different sensitivities, ulterior motives, and ideological climates in operation, the

> best advice is to remain open to clues in the individual setting (p. 17).

> A more complex performance may be required of you, along with more complex set of credentials, than formerly (p. 19).

Johnson (1975) is critical of traditional social science literature because it implies that gaining access involves purposive rational action and decision making only. The process is fraught with many uncertainties; responses from members can vary from gleeful acceptance to being thrown out on one's ear (p. 50).

He qualifies his own account as follows:

such an account necessarily emphasises the amount of rational calculation involved in gaining entry (p. 69).

It is best to emphasise at the outset that

playing it by ear is an essential continuing component of this phase of social research (p. 69).

Yet it is possible to extract a number of significant factors which have been identified by researchers in their accounts of access interactions.

Access is conceptualised here as a series of social encounters with members of the organisation when the researcher attempts to influence or exert power, in order that they become his allies and their organisation becomes his data source. The concept of power provides a useful link between various writings in this field, for aspects of power are what the researcher uses to achieve his initial goal of access.

The power aspect of access was highlighted for me during my first contact with the Social Services Department. In response to an outline of my requirements, the deputy director said that he and other members would need convincing of my worth:

we need to decide whether we've got the resources and whether you're worth it.

Access thus involved convincing organisational members of the researcher's worth. Field and action researchers are in a different power relationship with regard to organisations at the access phase of research because action researchers are often, though not invariably, invited in whereas field researchers are not. Invitations provide the action researcher with a power base. Thus whilst action research has been identified by, for example, Sofer (1961) and Thurley (1971), as a means of overcoming the problem of access, their `invited' status makes access unproblematic, and their power position in relation to the data source remains unexamined at this stage of the research process.

Field researchers, on the other hand, do refer to exerting influence, for example Geer (1970) and Delaney (1960). It is not the case, as Johnson (1975) states, that

> cunning and deception or other uses of power are never reported by field researchers as elements of their own activities (p. 56).

Power is used here to mean the ability to influence, rather than coerce. Goffman (1971) provides a useful expansion of the term power, which can be exercised by

> enlightenment, persuasion, exchange, manipulation, authority, threat, punishment or coercion (p. 234)

to direct the activity of others. He provides a pointer to the variety of processes whereby influence can be exerted, though he does not define his terms too closely.

In the main, field researchers rely on all but the last three methods referred to above. In particular, the use of deception and authority are two methods of influence which are frequently noted as being particularly useful. Additionally, their accounts refer to substantive issues in access negotiations, such as topic and method, as sources of influence. A distinction is infrequently drawn, though, between sources of influence, and how this influence is exerted. Below deception and authority as forms of influence are examined and how different types of influence may be exerted is considered.

Deception

Deception is defined as withholding information which will not facilitate the researcher's purpose. It is an aspect of Goffman's 'manipulation'(1971). The extent to which the researcher should, or indeed can, be open with subjects is debatable. Geer (1970) reports that though generally open, she and her research team pretended to have a hierarchical structure, with a 'head' who negotiated access with the organisation's administrative head. The pretence was thought to facilitate access. Johnson (1975) reports using deception in a number of areas: his experience, his purpose, his topic and his methodology. Thus he concocted experience, used a cover story, defocussed the research topic, and only revealed some of his methodological requirements after access had been obtained. Not surprisingly, Johnson believes that deception plays an important part in obtaining access: some of his requirements, if revealed initially, would have led to rejection. Additionally, until the researcher has access and some knowledge of the setting, he cannot be too specific about all his requirements.

In contrast, Beck (1970) suggests that

coming on straight is the best approach (p. 14).

As a rule

make explicit the terms of the bargain you are making

and do not try to gain access

without making a full disclosure (p. 15).

Whatever advantages accrue from deception will

come back to haunt you in later days (p. 15).

Delaney (1960) strikes something of a middle course:

the research proposal must be presented to responsible officials ... for the most part accurately ... we used a minimum of dissimulation (p. 452).

The dissimulation concerned the researcher's desired ideological posture; the impression was given that the researchers were ideological and politically on the organisation's side.

My own strategy was to be reasonably open. My growing interest in expenditure reductions was not made overt until members themselves expressed an interest. I was unsure of the effect of revealing my approach to a number of other organisations at the same time. It might for example, be construed as indicating a lack of commitment to their organisation. On the other hand it showed initiative and revealed that there were potential competitors for my services. I decided to be open for all these reasons and additionally because I was unsure of the inter-organisational and inter-departmental communications; any attempts to deceive might have led to discovery given my naivety.

Authority

As with deception, a number of substantive issues such as method and professional status are seen to be of use in providing the researcher with authority. Thus Geer (1970) built up the authority of her method by supplying examples of work were the same method had been used:

> the administrator should know that the researcher is not embarking on a fishing expedition; that a number of experienced social scientists have already made researches of this kind (p. 82).

Mauksh (1970), Beck (1970) and Johnson (1975) suggest that the researcher's position as a social scientist is most powerful in providing the authority that will facilitate access. Beck states that

> Generally the most effective method (of gaining access) is to be, and appear to be, a social scientist (p. 18)

This proves the

> best possible credentials (p. 14),

and is conveyed by using

> the evolved rhetoric of the social sciences (p. 14).

To present

the image of scientific respectability (p. 15)

is most effective. Johnson also believes in the magic of social science rhetoric, particularly in references and proposals. He refers to his use of

powerful symbols of academic respectability (p. 64),

and

social science rhetoric (p. 64).

Letters to the organisation where he was seeking access were written on university notepaper where

academic titles were used to lend academic respectability to the field researcher and the faculty sponsor, and phrases such as dedicated young scholar, reliable and trustworthy were used (p. 65).

He refers to these as the researcher's credentials. Rose (1970) recommends a letter of introduction detailing one's academic credentials, which he terms a letter of legitimacy. This of course assumes that social scientists and their work are viewed as being useful and valuable by organisational members. A number of author, such as Gill (1982) and Warmington (1980) suggest that this is not always the case: practising managers often react negatively and defensively to academics as 'theoreticians'.

In my experience the social science researcher was perceived and categorised as both academic and theoretical. A distinction was drawn between his and what was termed the practical. For example, during one access discussion, a financial comptroller said

I deal in pounds, shillings and pence, not concepts

with no apparent irony. For me the pound is just as much a concept as sub-culture, but for him it was not. A professional adviser in an Education department said she saw my work as 'academic rather than practical'. A Director of Civic Amenities said

33

we're a practical department; we're a `doing' not a `thinking' department.

Furthermore, these remarks were made in the context of my emphasising the practical, organisationally relevant nature of the work I wanted to do. Academic and practical were often seen as antonyms, and the researcher was consigned to the former category. This is perhaps, an example of defensive stereotyping, where the researcher is seen as a threat to current practice. Though action research is seen by authors such as Sofer (1961), Thurley (1971) and Rapoport (1970) to overcome problems of access, where there is no invitation, the offer of action research does not automatically open all doors in part because of member's views of the social sciences.

Authority also flows from the researcher's past work, or reputation. For example, Schein (1969) and Trist et al (1977) report that their reputations as action researchers facilitated access.

My own use of authority utilised my past work and academic experience, and my current status. I thus referred to my S.S.R.C. grant, and the C.N.A.A. as the registering body for my thesis, and obtained an 'academic' reference from my supervisor. As a research student I was conscious that my authority was not particularly high. By making explicit my association with various authoritative institutions, and my employment and academic history I endeavoured to remedy this weakness.

The above consideration of two forms of power, deception and authority, also indicated means by which power can be exerted, such a through methodological stance and academic status. A more comprehensive summary now follows.

Means of Influence

1)   Members' view of social science research: how far it is viewed as useful or a luxury (Scott: 1965), or a fringe service (Beck: 1970).

2) Researcher's background: how far his experience exerts a positive or negative influence. Gouldner (1954) suggests that similarity of experience with member facilitates access.

3) Academic status: the extent to which information about the researcher's funding body, academic institutions and references, post-school education and level of academic attainment exerts a positive or negative influence. Johnson (1975) suggests it is positive.

4) Topic: whether the topic has a positive or negative effect. Johnson (1975) and Delaney (1960) suggest that the topic can adversely affect access. Thus Delaney excluded certain controversial topics from his access discussions, on the assumption that they would be too threatening or too impractical. Because he subsequently found this assumption was open to question, he concluded:

> Certainly, organisational researchers should not toss prudence to the winds (in respect of research topic) but neither should they mistake it for timidity (p. 453)

5) Self presentation: Little (1970), Scott (1965), and Johnson (1975), all emphasise the importance of self presentation. Johnson (1975) and Delaney (1960) stress the importance of the researcher having

> skill in explaining his initial interest in terms which make sense to members of the setting (Johnson: p. 56).

6) Values: Beck (1970) suggests it is better to appear value free, whereas Delaney (1960) advises the researcher to support the official perspective.

7) Method: both Geer (1970) and Johnson (1975) stress the importance of methodology being seen as both appropriate and acceptable by those granting access.

8) Fore-knowledge: Johnson (1975), Geer (1970), Lawton (1970) and Delaney (1960) recommend researching the organisation prior to an approach for access.

In most areas of potential influence listed above, there is no certainty whether it will be positive or negative. The strength of the effect is also problematic. These issues serve to qualify the list of influencing behaviours which need further work to clarify their relative effect in particular cases.

Use of Allies

The purpose of exercising influence is to create allies within the organisation who will facilitate access in three ways: information-giving, supporting, and introducing. Dalton (1959) refers to the importance of allies. At an informational level, I was told by a member of one organisation who I should see and how to 'dress-up' my proposal to increase its chances of acceptance. Supporting can involve a stated agreement to the proposed access in written and verbal communication to other members. Thus my contact in the Social Service Department wrote to other managers there that he was

> sufficiently impressed with Mr. Frame to want to pursue the matter.

Additionally this memorandum served as my introduction to other members with whom I had access discussions.

Allies do not always perform a useful function though. On one occasion my request was refused in part because my ally was not highly regarded by senior management, nor had he provided me with an accurate picture of how the organisation worked. In the Social Services Department though, the use of allies was on the whole positive and allies who can exert a positive influence on the researcher's behalf are essential in obtaining access.

The action researcher is usually in a powerful position because he has allies if he is invited in. The majority of authors in this field state that they were invited in: Jacques (1951), Glidewell (1959), Tills (1961), Sofer (1961), Jones (1969), Clark (1972), Brown (1972), Henley (1975) and Foster (1972). There are apparent exceptions, such as Sadler and Barry (1970): they took the initiative but they too had powerful internal allies.

If researchers are invited in, it is more likely that members will have a positive view of the uses of social science research. As Sofer (1961) states, leading organisational members must realise

> that there is a relevant body of knowledge and category of people (social scientists) who may contribute to its (the problem) solutions (p. 121).

Given that a choice of consultant is made, it is more likely that some members will know and approve of his background, based on his reputation. Schein (1969) lists a number of reasons for clients contacting him: they have, for example, heard him lecture, or seen an article by him on the current problem. In fact, some sort of problem identification process will have taken place prior to a consultant being contacted. Tills (1969) suggests that

> the problem area has to be fairly well staked out before an appropriate consultant can be selected (p. 91)

and Sofer (1961) points out that

> work of this type cannot be set in motion unless the organisation contains leading members who realise that a problem exists (p. 121).

Issues of values will be less problematic because of the action researcher's reputation and professional stance. His methods too will have the authority attached to his reputation and the organisation will have decided to use resources and take some action on the issue. Organisational foreknowledge and self-presentation is less important because of the other factors listed above which exert a positive influence on the researcher's behalf.

Though the action researcher has a number of entry problems, these differ from those of the field researcher because of the former's power position in relation to members. For someone in the role of student, uninvited, with an interest in action, I found the work by authors in the field of action to be less helpful than it might have been, because, in general, access is assumed to be unproblematic. For field researchers this was not the case, and their accounts proved more useful.

My own strategy was to present myself to an organisation as a research resource, willing to examine a mutually agreed area and to produce something of practical value in return for data. This offer was of assistance in gaining access to the Social Services Department where their deputy director told me that they 'always insist on a quid pro quo' from the researcher. In the event, the mutually agreed topic of expenditure reductions became the major focus of this work.

Expenditure Reductions

Given the forms and sources of influence open to researchers, it is necessary to examine the place of expenditure reductions, both as a specific research topic, and generally as a determinant of how members will respond to research requests in other areas. Expenditure reductions were highlighted as a significant factor of organisational life in three of the six organisations I approached. Significantly they were also the three where I achieved more than an initial contact and learned something of the organisation itself.

As a topic, expenditure reductions was viewed both positively and negatively. In the Social Services Department the topic was suggested by my contact as being a useful area of study which was also the view of the majority of managers with whom I discussed access. Of eight managers, one was non-committal, and one was unenthusiastic. It was, he felt,

> too big; to sensitive. People are in the middle of coming to terms with the situation themselves.

This member, and the one who was non-committal, were both members of the F.W.M.T.. This team, as we shall see, experienced great difficulties in responding as directed to reductions management. For the majority of managers I spoke to, however, the topic was of positive value in facilitating access.

The term `sensitive' was also applied to expenditure reductions by a Chief Executive in another organisation approached. The Corporate Planning Unit for which he was responsible was enthusiastic about research which examined how different departments managed reductions. The Chief

Executive, on whose approval the research depended, was not, and he questioned me for about an hour on my motives and politics, my knowledge of Labour councillors and how I came to choose their organisation. The Financial Comptroller also joined in this questioning. Expenditure reductions were a sensitive and political issue, I was told, and they were not enthusiastic that it should be studied. There were strong implications from them of an undisclosed party political motive on my part, and access was refused.

In another organisation, the advent of expenditure reductions and responses to them were seen by the organisation's Director to preclude access for research in any topic. I was told that members would not co-operate. Their union had responded to impending resource reductions with a strategy of non-co-operation with management and co-operation would no be forthcoming for research either. Additionally, the government department to which the organisation was attached had decided that it was inadvisable to give researchers' access at a time of reductions. Thus openness to research was affected by the negative connotation of expenditure reductions.

Within the Social Services Department the resource demands made by a researcher at a time of stringency were raised by my first contact there, even before reductions as a topic was discussed.

> It's difficult enough providing services to clients, never mind time for researchers. We need to decide whether we've got the resources and whether you're worth it.

This suggests that at a time of reduced resources, members will think twice before using some of what remains to accommodate the researcher and will carefully evaluate research costs and benefits.

The topic of reductions and their management may facilitate or inhibit access, depending on members' views of the value of an outsider examining the issues involved. Access to research on other topics may be denied, or be vetted more rigorously than usual, at a time of resource pressure.

Summary

The purpose of this chapter was twofold. Firstly, it provided the reader with details of the epistemological perspective and the methodology. The work focuses on the actor's interpretation of events and his behaviour, as the basis for analysing expenditure reductions and sub-cultures. Interviews, observation and document analysis were used to elicit data. This was analysed in terms of the categories that emerged from the data, and a comparison with the relevant literature in this and allied fields. Secondly, the problem of access was examined using field and action researchers' accounts, in order to determine the sources and nature of influence that can be utilised by the researcher to facilitate access. The different power positions of the field and action researcher were noted.

Access at a time of expenditure reductions was examined, using data from three organisations, to determine whether this phenomenon facilitated or inhibited access. In general, access appears to be difficult. Where the topic specifically concerns reductions, members' responses will depend on whether they think such an examination would be of benefit to them or not.

3 Organisational monetarism

Introduction

This chapter provides a context with which data contained in subsequent chapters can be examined. Relevant literature is reviewed, and the concept of organisational monetarism in both its initial and elaborated form is analysed. Data on the instruction to managers to reduce resource expenditure is provided. Finally the terminology in use by managers to define reductions-related events is considered.

Literature

In general, literature is integrated with the data in this book. Some points which do not fit easily into this scheme are set out below. In particular a general theme which is found in studies in this area, and which I term organisational monetarism, is presented.

In the main, research of financial stringency focusses on the organisation as a whole, or the macro-level. For the purposes of this micro-level study, it is assumed that theory derived from the macro-level is relevant and applicable.

As previously noted, much of the work on expenditure reductions comes from settings in the public sector of the U.S.A. and, in particular, Higher Education. It is assumed that these studies are of relevance to work in an English Social Services Department, principally because their linking theme is the experience of managing financial stringency.

In Britain there has been much less research than in the U.S.A. in this field, though there are exceptions. For example, Judge (1978; 1981), Glennester (1980; 1981), and Ferlie (1980), examine resource decline in Social Services Departments. Fowler (1980), and the I.N.L.A.G.O.V. team (Wright: 1980) research local government's responses to scarce resources at a council-wide level. Davies and Morgan (1981), Pratt (1982), Sizer (1986), The Kogans (1983), and Gill and Pratt (1986) consider resource decline in Higher Education in the U.K.

Within the literature from both sides of the Atlantic there are a number of different foci used to examine resource decline. One is the structuralist perspective, which recommends an increase in rules and regulations as the solution to the problems presented by resource decline. For public organisations this often entails a move from a public to a private sector model of management, introducing, for example, cost effectiveness criteria. Examples of this approach are found in the work of Cyert (1979), Cazails (1979), and Pfeffer and Leblebici (1973). Authors such as Tolley (1980) and Sizer (1986) single out effective leadership as the solution to decline management. As alternative approach, represented by Scott (1976), may be termed the `human relations' solution. Here quantitative growth is replaced by qualitative growth, for example in increased self-awareness for individuals. One group of authors emphasise the unique position in which organisations and their managers find themselves when new skills are needed for new situations. The essays in Hirschhorn and Associates (1983), and work by Boulding (1975), and Levine (1978 and 1979), exemplify this approach. Some authors concentrate on financial management and the budgetary process as the means of dealing with decline: these include Green (1974), Pondy (1964), Ogden (1978), Dworak (1975) and Wolman with Davies (1980). Finally, authors such as Freeman and Hannan (1975), Pfeffer (1978), and Ford (1980) focus on organisational demography, the changes in the proportions of administrative and professional staff during decline. The uniting theme in this diversity is the expectation or observation that financial stringency will affect how an organisation is managed, and this is worthy of study.

Literature on redundancy, crisis and goals has been consulted. Redundancy literature which concentrates on the effects of impending layoffs, the management of such layoffs and the subsequent effects on those who remain with the organisation is relevant to this study. Gill (1975 a), and Woods (1980), are examples of this focus.

Crisis was a term used by some organisational managers to describe the effect of expenditure reductions. Hermann (1963), Billings et al (1980), and Staw et al (1981) all study the effect of crises on organisations. Whetton (1980: a & b), Murray and Jick (1985), and Gill and Pratt (1986) utilise the concept of crisis to analyse decline management, as does this study.

Following Merton (1957) a number of authors, including Warner and Havens (1968), explain resistance to change in terms of goal displacement. The link between behaviour and plurality of goals was significant in the organisation studied, and work by authors such as Frances and Stone (1956), Cohen (1965), and Cressey (1965), was therefore utilised.

Organisational Monetarism

The major theme emerging from both the literature and from pronouncements in the media by politicians or others on organisations and declining resources, is one I term organisational monetarism. This concept is implicit, and often in fact explicit, in the policy and practice of resource reduction.

Overall, organisational monetarism postulates a positive correlation between resource pressure and improved organisational efficiency and/or effectiveness. However, it assumes that managers are skilled and interested in financial management and cost control, use rational decision making processes which entail zero cost, can specify and quantify tasks and outcomes, and make positive innovations in response to stringency. These assumptions are examined in subsequent chapters by reference to empirical data. Here the concept is set out and examined in its initial and elaborated forms.

It may be argued that none of the elements of organisational monetarism are in themselves new, and do not therefore deserve to be distinguished by a specific label. It is, for example, merely the re-introduction of what Weber (1968) termed `formal rationality' under a new terminological guise. Organisational monetarism does incorporate the notion of formal rationality as the organising principle of bureaucracies. In particular it uses that aspect which emphasises quantification and, as Weber puts it, `calculation in monetary terms' (p. 86). But as Delaney (1963) points out, Weber did not study the decline of bureaucracies. What is new in this concept is the correlation between resource pressure and positive benefits, that is, the benefits of decline.

Organisational monetarism applies an economic hypothesis to the study of organisations. Within the discipline of economics, monetarism emphasises the benefit of reduced inflation which flows from the control and reduction of growth in the money supply. In organisational terms it suggest a causal connection between resource pressure and an increase in efficiency, or a reduction in waste. The benefits are therefore better resource use. Resources which are previously wasted will be used to make up the deficit caused by reductions, and the service will, it is assumed, be maintained.

The economist Donaldson (1982), describes the monetarist approach as follows:

> the basic tenet of monetarism is that inflation is caused by too much money (p. 23).

> Gradually to begin with, and then quite dramatically, governments became converted to the view that strict control of the money supply was the main weapon by which they should regulate the economy (p. 25).

> Limiting the growth in the quantity of money in the economy will be transmitted to lower inflation (p. 57).

Much the same description is provided by another economist, Harvey (1983):

> They (monetarists) assert that increases in the money supply can be directly related to extra spending and that therefore, much more attention must be directed to controlling increases in the supply of money (p. 106).

At the operational level, Donaldson (1982) describes the Government's attempts to control the money supply indirectly, by regulating the demand for money. One prong of this attack is

> trying to reduce the public sector's demand for money through expenditure cuts (p. 4).

At a theoretical level monetarism postulates the beneficial effects of controlling, or reducing the growth of, the money supply. At a practical level this is achieved by reducing demand.

That this economic approach was applied to organisations is apparent from political statements at ministerial level. For example, Mr. N. Ridley's comments on a reduction of forty-three million pounds in British Rail's grant from the Government were reported in both `The Guardian' and `The Standard' on October 25th. 1983. `The Guardian' reported that the Transport Secretary

> wanted a more efficient rail service, run with less money, which should be achieved without any major closures (p. 16).

`The Standard' quoted Mr. Ridley as saying British Rail would be

> better, more efficient and cheaper to run (p. 3).

That is, resource reductions were presented in the context of improving organisational efficiency. The Kogans (1983) in their discussion of reductions in Higher Education note that ministers were

> hopeful that a beneficial reconstruction of Higher Education would result from cuts (p. 39),

and quote an unnamed government spokesman's suggestion that

> universities should welcome reductions as an opportunity to reform themselves (p. 59).

The media noted the anticipated connection between less money and improvements. Thus 'The Guardian's' editorial (October 25th., 1983), on reductions in the National Health Service, described Mr. Norman Fowler, the Social Services Secretary as

> dressing up old-fashioned cuts as efficiency savings, which are assumed to be made after the budget is chopped and for which there is scant objective measure (p. 12).

Again then the tendency to establish a causal link between reduced resources and efficiency is apparent.

This positive correlation is stated succinctly by Glennester (1980):

> the more stern the financial climate, the more rationally organisations will react (p. 368).

Similarly Caiden (1980) states:

> Common sense suggests that if officials and politicians have fewer resources at their disposal, they will have to accomplish objectives more efficiently (p. 135).

Though neither author supports this linkage, there are a number of writers including Bogue (1972) and McTighe (1979) who do.

As Judge (1981) tells us, a positive correlation is seen as the silver lining surrounding the cuts cloud. He quotes Glennester's (1981) summary of this position as follows:

> Without a regular increment to distribute, it is argued that local authorities will be forced to consider their base spending and make hard choices. It will become more important to consider the relative effectiveness of different programmes or activities. Authorities and professionals will be forced to question the purpose of things they traditionally do. Services will emerge as from a health farm, toned up, slimmed down and altogether more effectively planned and co-ordinated. (Glennester p. 50).

Though the author is acting as devil's advocate, it is a useful summary of the optimistic view of the effects of financial reductions. It is interesting for two reasons: it identifies the dietary focus of reductions-related symbols, and focusses attention on the process of spending reviews as the essential link between resource pressure and efficiency.

Dietary Symbolism

The use of dietary symbols with reference to organisations experiencing resource pressure is noted, though not examined, by Caiden (1980) in the context of reductions resulting from tax revolts in the United States.

> In the rhetoric of the tax revolts, slim is beautiful (p. 135).

> The image of the lean and purposeful organisation is compelling (p. 136).

Levine (1978) identifies two examples of what he terms

> official cutback rhetoric: `cut the fat' and `tighten our belts' (p. 319).

Whilst such symbolism is not in itself new, its application to the context of reductions in public sector resources is worth considering because it can be seen both as an `explanation' and as a justification of the theory/practice of organisational monetarism.

The symbolism is dietary, and uses opposing concepts of desirable and undesirable states, such as healthy/unhealthy, fit/unfit, and lean/fat. An analogy is drawn between the human body and the organisation. The terms used and the values attached to them are transposed from the body to the organisation. The process whereby the desirable state is achieved is slimming (operating with reduced calories) or resource reduction (operating with fewer resources). Undesirable overconsumption thereby becomes correct consumption, and the process is identified, in a commonsense way, by terms such as `slimming down'.

47

The meaning contained in these symbols is contestable on the following grounds. Lean or thin is not always an indication of good health. It may be due to poverty, or ill health. In extreme cases it may be due to anorexia nervosa. Were this to be the case, any claim to causal connection with good health would be a contradiction. The important stage of diagnosis has been left out. Similarly, fat is not always caused by overconsumption. Moreover the body and the organisation are not as similar as is implied. Only two factors, height and weight, are used to determine the desirable state of the body. Both of these are easily measurable. Organisations are far more complex than the analogy suggests, and organisational theorists are as yet in no position to formulate a chart, similar to that devised by the medical profession which indicates the range of desirable weight in relation to height.

By focusing on one factor, consumption, and ignoring the particular circumstances of this consumption, dietary metaphors ignore the complexity of the issue. They assume that there is 'organisational fat' in all public organisations. Potthoff (1975), for example, tells us

> Don't fool yourself into believing you have no fat to cut. Everyone has it. Cut away (p. 14).

Behn (1980) on the other hand, remarks that

> it would be nice if retrenchment could be managed by cutting the fat. And advocates of budgetary reductions can argue that this is all that is required. Wonderful if it can be done. In many situations, however, such a miracle is not possible (p. 614).

The use of dietary symbols assumes an agreed definition of what organisational 'fat' is. Biller (1980) equates organisational 'fat' with 'organisation slack' (Cyert and March: 1963). Potential benefits of 'slack', such as flexibility and conflict reduction (Biller: 1980, and Levine et al: 1981), are not recognised by organisational monetarism.

The Reduction Process

Organisational monetarism further assumes the process of reduction will be unproblematic and have zero cost, based on the belief that organisations are formally rational. Chapters 5 - 8 detail the difficulties experienced by managers of one organisation and indicate the nature and extent of costs involved. A number of authors including some who support organisational monetarism, refer to the costly nature of the reductions management process, identifying pressure both on resources and intra-organisational relations. Thus Davies and Morgan (1981) who adopt a stance in support of the concept, point out that

> to develop and implement a more rational pattern of reductions instead of an arbitrary one would require several years (p. 11).

Balderston (1972) suggests that

> These approaches (a concern with output measurement and productivity improvements) will take a great deal of time, money, and above all, courage (p. 26-27).

In referring to resource allocation, Pondy (1970) and David (1979) suggest that information costs are not zero, and Pratt (1982) asserts

> Any system to allocate resources must not in itself be disproportionately expensive. It would be salutary for example to assess the hidden costs of the time given by all the academic staff and officials to the U.G.C. and N.A.B. (p. 137).

Hirschhorn (1983b) refers to the expansion

> of managerial and planning costs (p. 115).

in retrenchment. Thus 'costs' result both from decision making on how to reduce expenditure, and from the operation of post-reductions control mechanisms. Assuming that productive intra organisational relations are a resource, there is a cost here too.

Organisational monetarism also assumes ease of task measurement, known and desired end states, and a causal relationship between scarcer resources and organisational health.

Resource Pressure and Increased Efficiency

Resource pressure, it has been suggested, leads to increased efficiency, because it necessitates a review and evaluation of all spending. For example, Stewart (1980) predicts resource pressure will result in a move from incremental to zero based budgeting because

> In a period of standstill, room for manoeuvre can only be created by examining existing resource allocation. This will involve a much wider scrutiny of resources and a much longer budgetary review (p. 20).

> New needs can only be met in so far as existing resources can be used in new ways (p. 21).

Biller (1980) indicates that

> Retrenchment makes possible the redeployment of resources (p. 605).

March and Cohen (1974) observed an initial period of confusion following by improved decision making as an outcome of fewer resources. Bogue (1972) suggests reductions result in institutional review and intense introspection. Greenwood et al (1980) noted a tendency for local authorities to move from a `political' to a `rational' model of resource decision making, as a result of stringency. This was, however, only temporary and during the following year they found continued stringency and reduced rationality. Ferlie (1980) prescribes the fostering of innovative schemes as imperative

> if an authority wishes to meet the changing balance of needs and resources in a full cost-effective way (p. 1).

In the education field, Cheit (1971 and 1973) refers to the beneficial and desirable effects of stringency. He discovered a positive correlation over time between financial stringency and improved management processes, such as budgetary controls and planning committees.

The Carnegie Foundation (1975) notes an increase in

> administrative muscle - to shift resources and make better use of them (p. 6.)

And Davies and Morgan (1981) believe that

> fiscal uncertainty and stress can be a creative force for change, particularly programmatic reformulations, within institutions of Higher Education (p. 63).

Tichy (1980) states that

> cutbacks on grants forced the centre to be more efficient in the provision of health care and to demonstrate cost effectiveness (p. 167).

Financial stringency thus leads to efficient resource utilisation via a review of all spending, and the improvement of processes for carrying out such reviews.

Resource Pressure and Decreased Efficiency

In contrast to the above, a number of authors note that financial stringency results in decreased efficiency in respect of less effective decision making, an increased use of power, increased conflict, pressure against change and goal displacement.

Ferlie and Judge (1980) regard the optimistic view of reductions as based on a rational model of budgeting. They concluded that

> confusion and uncertainty were more in evidence in the fiscal experience of most Social Services Departments than substantive steps in the direction of a more rational and synoptic base searching (p. 2).

The quality of Social Services Departments' decision making therefore has been one casualty of the shift from growth to retrenchment (p. 29).

In relation to a particular decision area they say policy

owes everything to opportunism and administrative expediency and virtually nothing to rationality (p. 24).

Bebbington and Ferlie (1980) make the same point. Caiden (1980) suggests that

Politicians and officials may not accommodate fiscal stress by restricting expenditure, scaling down objectives to fit fiscal realities (p. 154).

Based on a review of scarcity and budgeting in pre-revolutionary (1789) France, she suggested that fewer resources do not lead to improved financial management, but rather the reverse.

Hills and Mahoney (1978) observe that resource pressure results in a move from a bureaucratic to a political model of decision making, and Pfeffer (1978) notes a correlation between fewer resources and a greater use of power in the decision making process. March and Simon (1958) connect resource decrease with increased intra organisational conflict and competition. Manns and March (1978) report that university departments with the strongest reputations are least responsive to changes demanded by financial adversity. Since reputation is a source of power both in itself, and because it produces finance, this power is used to resist change.

Cheit (1973) noted that

several colleges point out that financial stress also creates pressure against change (p. 64).

in the direction outlined above, though only in a minority of cases. The Carnegie Foundation (1975) states that early responses to reduced resources on campuses were largely negative:

one finds disappointment, conflict, fear of rigidity (p. 11).

Wolman with Davies (1980) suggest that one of the most common and successful strategies to deal with fiscal pressure is

> to reduce by inaction (p. 244)

With steady-state budgets, inflation rather than action by managers results in reductions. Rubin (1980) states that there is no automatic connection between less money and improved financial management; a strong authority structure and budgetary flexibility are pre-requisites of such a change. In the absence of these, she states

> retrenchment cannot be carried out (p. 175).

Attempts to do so

> will produce strangely ineffective results and paralyse the organisations involved (p. 175).

Frances and Stone (1956) concern themselves with the practices of a public sector employment bureau. They report that

> the constant pressure to cut the budget (p. 136),

resulted in an emphasis on productivity reporting, as a security or defensive device, to the detriment of the job finding service. This type of goal-deplacement is also noted by Cohen (1965). Staw and Szwajkowski (1975) noted an increase in illegal acts by companies as their resources fell.

Finally, in her earlier work, Rubin (1976 and 1977) indicates that as a result of stringency and the accompanying uncertainty,

> some aspects of decision making improved, whilst other deteriorated (1977: p. 254).

Thus the picture that emerges from the literature is contradictory both in terms of whether or not improvements are noted and whether these are apparent in the short or long term.

Organisational Monetarism Elaborated

The elaboration of organisational monetarism focusses analytical attention on the absence in practice of the predicted innovations. It dismisses the positive changes reported above, such as greater efficiency (Tichy: 1980) and tighter budgetary controls (Cheit: 1971 and 1973) as conservative, not innovative, responses and re-defines innovation as `doing things differently' (Whetton: 1981). Lack of innovative activity is explained by reference to characteristics of the resource loss. In summary, it suggests that the larger and quicker the cut, the greater the chance of innovation.

Examples of this elaboration of organisational monetarism are found in studies by both Murray and Jick (1985) and Gill and Pratt (1986). They explain, at the macro-level, the absence of innovatory responses to financial stringency by directing attention to characteristics of the stringency itself, and in particular, the size of the reduction and the speed with which it takes place. A distinction is drawn, based on the model provided by Zammuto and Cameron (1982), between slow erosion and dramatic decline. More innovatory behaviour is anticipated if reductions are large and speedy than if they are small and slow. Large and speedy reductions generate a greater sense of crisis, and necessity is seen as the mother of innovation. Thus organisational monetarism is refined by moving from a position where reduction in general will be beneficial, to one where particular characteristics of reductions are seen to trigger positive responses. Before examining this causal connection, it is necessary to define the responses involved: efficient/effective and conservative/innovative.

Whetton (1981) provides a useful summary in his macro-level analysis of educational institutions; he suggests that private organisations, spurred by competition, use times of resource plenty to innovate, that is, to alter the mix of their activities, and make

a shift in the services provided or the clients served (p. 83).

This strategy is termed the `effectiveness option'. In time of scarcity, the private sector will focus on increasing efficiency:

scarcity is the time to live off the organisation's fat, and not waste precious resources experimenting with new ideas (p. 92).

This conservative response is termed the `efficiency option' (p. 83). In contrast, public sector organisations use times of plenty to do more of the same, and they respond to scarcity by doing less of the same, that is, increasing or decreasing current programmes. They are unlikely to innovate whatever their financial circumstances. For Whetton, scarcity should provide incentives for public sector organisations to innovate:

The key to enhancing the adaptive potential of these organisations is utilising the pressure of scarcity to spur innovation (p. 92).

In analysing their field data, both Murray and Jick (1985), and Gill and Pratt (1986) link lack of innovation (the efficiency option) with moderate levels of stringency. Thus in respect of British polytechnics, Gill and Pratt (1986) `believe a crucial, underlying factor' (p. 2), which elicited the efficiency rather than the effectiveness response, was the nature of resource pressure: erosion or small reduction over a number of years, rather than a sudden crisis, involving large scale resource loss. Murray and Jick (1985) analyse the lack of innovation in a sample of six American hospitals. They refer to `the absence of major cuts' (p. 121), and the presence of `moderate cutbacks' (p. 111), `moderate financial constraints' (p. 117) and `moderate long term squeeze' (p. 117).

In general, as would be consistent with a moderate level of crisis, efforts were made to save money only by relatively traditional attempts at increased internal efficiency (p. 119).

In contrast, they suggest that

had the decline been more severe or sudden (p. 118),

more radical changes may have occurred. This analysis raises questions of what a large/major reduction, or a small/moderate cutback is, and of whose definitions are in use. It also questions whether organisations can invariably be expected to respond innovatively to crisis, and why any response other than the efficiency one was expected.

The definition of the significance of size was provided by the authors, rather than members of the organisation studied. Thus Murray and Jick (1985) state:

> It is significant that, in objective terms, the crisis represented by funding cuts was moderate. Budget increments ranged from 1% to 4.6% below the level in inflation (p. 117).

Yet Staw et al (1981) states that either

> incremental or radjcal environmental change can cause threat to an entity (p. 519).

Given Murray and Jick's purpose of linking organisational responses to characteristics of decline, the notion of objective terms is unlikely to be relevant. It would have been useful if members perception on this issue were known, that is, whether the `objective' definition of the phenomena as moderately acceptable reflected the views of those who managed the organisations studied, or whether they regarded the issue as one of major importance. In the absence of this data, the material presented by Murray and Jick could be analysed in terms of the literature on crisis, and therefore without reference to the identified characteristics of decline.

Some analyses of organisational responses to crisis suggest that the advent of crisis does not necessarily produce the type of innovatory responses predicted by, for example, Whetton (1981). In fact Whetton acknowledges that whilst in theory, public sector organisations should use the stimulus of retrenchment to explore new opportunities (the effectiveness option), in practice they do not do this. He identifies a number of `deeply entrenched organisational dynamics' (p. 91), which militate against innovation. He offers a prescription for how organisations should respond to financial crisis then, rather than describing the actual behaviour of organisations.

Staw et al (1981) similarly offer a prescription for organisations facing the threat of financial stringency, but suggest that in practice organisations respond to the threat not with innovation but with rigidity, that is, the `efficiency option'. The same point is made by Hermann (1963). Ford

(1981) also provides a prescription for coping with crisis after noting a number of organisational dynamics such as 'group think', whereby organisations contribute to their own crisis. Holsti (1978) suggests that crisis impares coping mechanisms, rather than becoming the mother of innovation. Thus organisations do not inevitably respond to crisis by innovating. One could argue that the lack of innovation noted by Murray and Jick (1985) resulted from organisational dynamics of the type referred to by Whetton (1981) and Staw et al (1981), rather than the nature of the reduction itself.

Finally, both Gill and Pratt (1986), and Murray and Jick (1985), in referring to conditions of 'slow erosion', utilise the model of responses to decline devised by Zammuto and Cameron (1982). This model, based on research into the American car industry, defined two sources of decline, one a decrease in finances due to reduced demand, and the other a shift in the organisation's domain, based on a change in demand for types of goods or services offered. They suggest that where decline results from a drop in resources, whether this is slow erosion or unexpected contraction, the outcome will be an emphasis on efficiency. Only where there is a shift in the shape of the organisation's environment, such as a change in demand for products or services, will the effectiveness option be considered. That there was no such environmental shift in the institutions researched by Murray and Jick (1985) is clearly stated:

> the sphere of the hospital's environment was not changing.
> For example, there was no significant change in the
> characteristics of the population served (p. 117).

In these conditions Zammuto and Cameron (1982) predict efficiency responses, irrespective of whether the reductions are continuous or unexpected. Thus lack of innovation can be analysed in terms of the source of decline, irrespective of whether it was slow erosion or unexpected contraction. Innovation, or the effectiveness option, will only be considered by organisations when there is a

> qualitative change in the type of performance an
> organisation can engage in (Zammuto and Cameron: p. 250).

The predicted connection therefore between sudden reductions and innovatory behaviour still remains open to question. The size of the reduction did not form part of Zammuto and Cameron's analysis.

Both Glassberg (1978) and Sizer (1986) consider size of reduction as a variable in determining organisational responses, but both qualify their analysis by reference to other significant variables. Glassberg (1978) suggests that size and permanence of reduction are significant in determining responses. He distinguishes between incremental reductions (small and temporary) and quantum decreases (substantial and permanent). As an example of quantum decreases he refers to a 20.8 per cent reduction in the New York City work force between 1975 and 1977. Creative responses and risk-taking are more likely with quantum reductions, whereas incremental reductions elicit traditional responses, such as cost cutting. However, innovation is only likely when organisational leaders have decided that a defensive strategy, such as cutting the most popular services, will no longer be effective in maintaining their own reputations and interests. Thus members' perceptions of the permanence of reductions, as well as their size, are significant here.

Sizer (1986), in a survey of nine British universities, links both size of reduction and effective leadership to innovatory response. Thus institutions such as Salford, which experienced large reductions, came up with significant innovatory responses, such as attracting finance and support from industry. On the other hand Bradford, which also experienced large cuts, did not innovate to any degree. Most of Sizer's sample `felt severely limited in their capacity to innovate' (p. 3). In this particular case what differentiates institutions in respect of innovatory behaviour is, in addition to other subsidiary factors, the style of leadership.

Thus on examination, those who support a refined version of organisational monetarism are found either to qualify this with other variables (Sizer: 1986; Glassberg: 1978), to offer the notion as a prescription (Whetton: 1981; Staw et al: 1981), or to make contestable assumptions both about the definition of size and organisational responses to crisis (Murray and Jick: 1985; Gill and Pratt: 1986). Thus a direct linkage between size/speed and response is open to question. This is not to suggest that the size of reductions is insignificant, but rather that this significance is located in members' perceptions of size. It is the contention of this research that size was less significant than organisational factors of sub-culture and context in determining managerial response.

The Introduction of Reductions

The strategies and justifications reported in the following chapters took place within the general context of instructions to the Department, from local councillors, to recommend reductions in resource consumption, but to continue to provide services despite these reductions. Overall, expenditure reductions were presented to managers in financial rather than service terms, as a resource-led, rather than a service-led process. Specific instructions related to money and the percentage by which this was to be reduced; references to service delivery were far less specific.

On two occasions the Department was instructed to review its budget, and recommend expenditure reductions on a percentage basis. The first involved the current budget and the second, the estimated budget for the following year. On the first occasion the D.M.T. instructed middle, or third-tier, managers to prepare a list of reduction recommendations in line with instructions the D.M.T. had received. As this information was classified as confidential, there was no interdivisional consultation between the organisation's two middle management teams. On the second occasion, middle managers were again asked to make recommendations. These were presented to a meeting of all middle managers. On both occasions, the D.M.T. considered recommendations, and made changes or additions before forwarding them to councillors. These events took place in the second half of 1979.

When the annual budget was approved in April 1980, two-thirds of the sum the D.M.T. had recommended to be taken from F.W.'s budget was `added back'. Despite this, the F.W. division had to deal with a larger reduction than the R. and D.C. division. In particular ten per cent of posts were left vacant, a `managed vacancy element', compared to 5.6 per cent in R. and D.C.. Members of F.W.M.T. felt that they had done badly out of the exercise compared to R. and D.C., though not as badly as had been anticipated. Most members of R. and D.C. felt they had `done well' or `had not been much affected'.

59

During this period of decision making, councillors were seen to have created uncertainty. First they decided to make reductions; this decision was then reversed; and then the decision was reinstated and reductions again became Council policy. Similarly the percentage by which the budget was to be reduced varied. As one D.M.T. member said, it was a

> scenario built on shifting sand: first it was five per cent, then seven per cent, then three and a half per cent.

That is, changes in the anticipated amount of the reduction was a major source of uncertainty.

Senior management passed the instructions they had received on to middle managers. These were not presented in terms of specific service priorities, with low priority areas first in line for reductions, but as a percentage reduction in divisional budgets. Additional points made by councillors were passed to middle managers:

(a) there would be no redundancies;

(b) there would be no development of service without compensatory savings;

(c) councillors would abide by manifesto pledges;

(d) budgets could not be overspent.

In addition, managers were told there were to be `no sacred cows' or automatically protected areas, and were invited to recommend reductions in other divisions as well as their own. Beyond this, managers were left to their own devices to decide what to recommend for reduction.

Although one senior manager said

> Local Government is cushioned from the most dramatic effects of cuts as their policy is no redundancies,

managing expenditure reductions was still seen to be problematic. One aspect of this problem concerned the different realities which were seen to be imposed by expenditure reductions and which are reflected in the terms used to describe them.

Terminology in Use

The following terms were used to describe expenditure reductions and activities associated with them: `the cuts'; `expenditure allocation'; `expenditure re-allocation'; `revenue re-allocation'; `re-allocation of resources'; `negative growth'; and `no growth'.

Of these seven, `the cuts' was by far the most popular term: it was used most frequently by the majority of managers. It was used to define a number of activities associated with expenditure reductions such as recommending reductions in spending, increasing revenue by, for example, implementing charges for services, and managing the effects of reductions. The term does not convey specifically what was to be cut; it does not focus either on financial resources or service delivery. Rather it focusses on the reduction aspect, conveying a general impression of a climate of loss in a dramatic form, the term `cuts' having far more impact than `reductions'. There was little debate on the usage of this popular term; it has in fact, passed into common usage with the public. On one occasion a middle manager referred to other terms used to describe expenditure reductions as

the latest organisational euphemism for the cuts.

This suggests that there was a certain amount of conscious evaluation of terminology amongst some members. The extent to which the remaining six terms can be classified as euphemisms is now examined.

These six terms were less popular: they were in the main used by senior managers rather than other groups. Four of the terms focus specifically on financial resources, by reference to `revenue' or `expenditure'. Thus the reality of expenditure reductions is defined in financial terms and the `solution' relies on the manipulation of financial resources. These terms ignore the decrease-in-resources aspect of the situation and imply a steady-state financial position. They also ignore service delivery and the non-financial aspects of the management task, both of which are influenced by resource reductions. Thus defined, the problem becomes restricted to the area of financial management alone rather than encompassing wider and more sensitive issues such as reduction or withdrawal of service.

The other two terms, `negative' and `no growth', could refer either to services or expenditure. Using such terms dilutes the negative value attached to `no' and exploits the positive connotations of `growth'. Thus `no growth' conveys a different and less pessimistic impression than `the cuts'. In the same way `negative growth' is a more positive term than `decline'.

Each of these terms can be used euphemistically where the intention is to manipulate the reality of the situation. Certainly, the use of all terms except `the cuts' limits a consideration of the full implications of the changes on those affected. On the other hand the way in which senior managers were presented by councillors with demands for percentage reductions in their budgets did not recognise the implications for service delivery. Rather than differing motives it is the differing realities presented by the terms which are significant: the majority of terms in use define the expenditure reductions task as one of financial management alone.

Summary

In this chapter the literature on organisations and expenditure reductions was reviewed. The concept of organisational monetarism was highlighted as a link between much of the work in this area. Organisational monetarism proposes a positive correlation between fewer resources and improved organisational efficiency or effectiveness.

The economic theory of monetarism was set out, and how it has been applied to organisations noted. Organisational monetarism was questioned on a number of grounds. The dietary images in use were found to contain a number of assumptions. The notion of the `fat' organisation for example was not found to be universally accepted. Similarly the assumption of zero-cost was contested. The link between size/speed of reductions and positive innovation was critically examined.

The instructions on expenditure reductions issued to managers were outlined. Finally the differing realities underlying the terms expenditure reductions were described.

4 Management sub-cultures

Introduction

This chapter introduces the concept of managerial sub-cultures: it examines their maintenance, elaboration, content, and function.

After noting the connection between structure and culture, and identifying the limited usage of the term culture amongst managers, five levels of typification of management team sub-cultures are elaborated. Three dimensions of difference between the two middle management teams, R. and D.C. and F.W. are then identified: consultation, speed of decision making, and the significance of formal structure. The variety within a group's sub-culture, and the external awareness of this variety is then examined. A comparison is made between each group's construction of routine and critical issues, followed by the effects on cultural maintenance of interaction between groups. The process of the middle management teams is then differentiated. From this analysis, the function of sub-culture is deduced. Finally the sub-culture of the Director's management team (D.M.T.) is described.

A sub-cultural perspective aids understanding of stringency management because it exposes and partially accounts for differences between management groups, and compares these groups in respect of behaviour and values. Observable differences in managerial activities and attitudes to expenditure reductions in part reflect the influence of collective 'taken for granted' assumptions of the sub-cultures of different management groups. Thereby, the analysis of managerial response is not solely linked either to characteristics (such as size) of the reduction itself, nor to issues of financial management which result from classifying the phenomena of resource reductions as of 'financial' significance only. Group values were, in fact, frequently used by members to analyse or account for their own and other managers' behaviour. Thus a sub-cultural explanation was of significance to managers in interpreting reduction related issues.

The organisation's two middle management teams were the principle source of data. The definition of sub-culture used is set out in Chapter I: a group's typification or 'taken for granted' ways of thinking and working which need to be known as a pre-requisite for acceptance as a competent member.

Culture and Structure

Authors such as Jaques (1951) have, in their analyses, separated culture and structure. Clark (1974) suggests that these are the same phenomena looked at from different perspectives. Though the focus of this research is culture, that is not to argue that structure is unimportant, but rather to locate structure in the context of how culture is seen to operate within the organisation. Structure defines the formal hierarchy of grades, and divisional organisation of tasks, as represented by the organisational chart, and is therefore relevant in two ways.

Firstly, management groupings, or teams, were determined by the formal organisational structure. Each team was seen to have its own sub-culture. Other possible groupings based on factors such as age or professional qualifications were not identified by managers. The divisional structure of the organisation and the ensuing isolation was seen by managers to encourage rather than discourage the maintenance of different and distinctive patterns between groups.

Secondly, the distinction between structure and culture was reflected in the dimensions used by managers to identify particular cultural traits. A significant aspect of the 'taken for granted' view of both R. and D.C.M.T. and D.M.T. was that structural position should determine behaviour and values. In particular, being a third-tier manager was constructed to mean accepting the task of managing expenditure reductions. Structure was generally perceived to be a more significant aspect of the R. and D.C.M.T. sub-culture than of the F.W.M.T. sub-culture.

Since sub-cultures are taken for granted, the organisational analyst, whether member or researcher, faces the problem of how to become aware of the sub-cultures that are current. A group's sub-culture is not written down in, for example, the manner of a job description or organisational chart.

In this particular organisation there were very occasional references to 'value differences' in the minutes of meetings. These were not however elaborated. Only two managers actually used the term 'culture', although throughout the research period managers did refer to phenomena, but used other terms.

Culture

A F.W. manager referred to the F.W.M.T.'s culture in the context of

> a right and wrong attitude to the cuts. The functional one - do it because we're employees - would not get much of a positive response at F.W.M.T., because of the group's culture.

Culture here influences the selection of presented attitudes via members' knowledge of culturally defined 'right' and 'wrong'. Incorrect or wrong attitudes are unlikely to be presented because of a negative response. The member was sure the group had a culture, which involved unchallenged notions of 'right' and 'wrong' attitudes and related action. Culture here provided moral guidance.

For an R. and D.C. manager, culture meant

> a pattern of working together as a team, an approach to supervision, accepted and unwritten ways of doing things. A

65

leader's style is pre-ordained by the culture of his area. They (F.W.M.T.) wouldn't have anyone who did not believe in the consultative process.

He went on to say that

R. and D.C.M.T. don't have a common culture, there's no cohesiveness. There's no common interest and therefore no common culture. In some parts of the service there is cohesion, they think as a group.

Culture was then apparent for this member, but not in relation to his own management team. It comprised of unwritten ways of action and attitudes, and was made apparent by group members abiding by these - `thinking as a group'. It was perpetuated through selection.

Nevertheless, this member was able to generalise about his own management team, R. and D.C.M.T., in terms of appearance and life-style, and used the former as a symbol of management style. He described his colleagues as `fuddy duddy' and referred particularly to their style of dress (formal suits, collars and ties), their age (old), and their home circumstances:

living in a large house in Buckinghamshire with a large car and garden.

For him, a relaxed, informal appearance, such as jeans and long hair, symbolised a relaxed or democratic management style. By contrast he pointed to his own formal appearance, and identified his management style as `directive': he was a `democratic dictator'. Interestingly, this approach to management was one that he shared unknowingly with his R. and D.C. colleagues. Using these dimensions he said

in F.W.M.T. there's one person more like the R. and D.C. lot, from his age and image: solid and conformist.

Dress was not generally used by other members to symbolise groups, though the data on formality and informality of dress was confirmed by observation of management team meetings. Members of each middle management team did characterise management styles in terms of the directed/democratic dichotomy used above. Though generally unacknowledged there was then a connection between appearance and attitudes.

Typification

On the basis of members' discussions, it is possible to distinguish five levels of specificity in their typification of group sub-culture. The first level was the least specific, the meaning being almost totally taken for granted. The fifth level was the most specific, where taken for granted features were exposed.

The first level of least specificity was observed during management team meetings of both F.W. and R. and D.C., where the very mention of the other team, who were not present, was sufficient to produce derisory sniggers or sympathetic nods. This indicated a shared,but unstated meaning of the symbols `F.W.M.T.' and `R. and D.C.M.T.'.

At the next level of specificity, members sometimes described a particular perspective on an issue by reference to a management team symbol. Thus reference was made to `the F.W. view' by members of both management teams. That is, group members were seen to hold a common view, or `think as a group' to quote the R. and D.C. manager referred to above, though what these `views' were remained unstated. Similarly in describing his attitude to reductions a F.W. manager said

I'm nearer R. and D.C. on this.

He went on to expand what this meant. Nevertheless, the group was symbolised as having a particular attitude, and the symbol R. and D.C. was used to describe it.

More specific still were references to different `philosophies of management' and `different ways of coming at the world' as an explanation for responses to reductions. These were used by a R. and D.C. manager and a F.W. manager respectively. Minutes of a meeting where the two groups discussed their differences, referred to `anxieties about philosophical and management styles' between the two groups. Reference was also made to a F.W. manager who does not feel her attitudes are shared by R. and D.C.,

and to an R. and D.C. manager remarking that

there seems to be a different political attitude to the cuts.

At this level of specificity, group differences were characterised in terms of `philosophical and management styles' and `attitudes'. What these styles and attitudes were was not usually stated; there was a taken for granted acceptance of share, but unstated meaning.

At a fourth level meanings were elaborated to some extent by members defining these styles. Thus F.W. managers' generally described the style of management prevalent in their division as `participative and democratic' and `participative and consultative'.

In F.W., the taken for granted is consensus management.

Similarly the R. and D.C. team described their management style as that of a `benign despot'. With reference to the issue of expenditure reductions, an R. and D.C. manager said F.W. managers were concerned with the

philosophical implications. We are more practically orientated as individuals and as a group.

Even if individual members did not subscribe to these typifications, they were nevertheless aware of their existence. Thus one F.W. manager said

others in F.W.M.T. imply R. and D.C. is less democratic, following instructions from a higher level with no discussion: it's less open and consultative.

Group typifications were most specific - the fifth level of specificity - when interactions between members of each management team were discussed. Managers identified a number of dimensions of difference between the two groups: the consultation process, the speed of decision making, and the significance of formal structure.

Consultation

F.W. managers believed they were not consulted sufficiently by their R. and D.C. colleagues. The following quotation represents the F.W. view of the consultative process as it operated both in their own division and in R. and D.C.. A F.W. manager said he and his colleagues felt

> left out (by R. and D.C.M.T) of important issues affecting us.
> R. and D.C. is less good at consulting.

A contrast was made with his own division:

> F.W. operates the other way; consultation takes years, it's cumbersome, but everyone is involved.

F.W.'s perceived and expressed culture was, according to another manager

> consultative and participative; let everyone have a say; circulate documents for comments.

R. and D.C. was said by this member to have staff who were

> passive, accepting and do as they're told.

She contrasted this attitude with that of F.W. staff, who were used to `questioning' and `expected to participate'. Here we have a dimension with consultation and participation at one end, and passive acceptance at the other. It was used for both management styles and staff expectations by members of F.W.M.T., who aligned themselves to the consultative/participative style. F.W. thus saw itself as consultative and R. and D.C. as directive. No F.W. member symbolised F.W. as directive, and R. and D.C. as participative.

The R. and D.C. perspective on consultation was that whilst some was useful, action was more important. In certain cases action had to be taken quickly. Their team leader said

I believe in organisational democracy but prefer to be a despot and take decisions on my own say so. I don't like to consult, it takes a long time.

He referred to R. and D.C.

having to participate (with F.W.M.T) in an ongoing, undirected consultation which might bugger up its plans.

Here a distinction was drawn between consultation and being directed, which is similar to the F.W. dimension referred to above. Consultation is regarded as dysfunctional, as it results in delays and the amending of plans. F.W. required

consultation on everything .... but you can't consult about everything

as one R. and D.C. manager put it. In the presence of F.W. managers, an R. and D.C. member said

R. and D.C. sometimes get on with it, rather than consult. Some decisions require immediate action.

Another said

In some cases if it's a choice between do and talk, we do.

Here a distinction was made between consultation/talk and action. Consultation was thus not seen as always being an integral and useful part of action by R. and D.C.M.T. managers. The distinction between doing and talking was used by R. and D.C. managers to differentiate themselves from F.W. managers. F.W. was said by an R. and D.C. manager to use meetings to

deal with their anxieties. F.W. spend hours analysing and acknowledging feelings. We cannot afford the time. We're frustrated by meetings, there's too much to do, we have to look after the kids (in care). We need more doing in this service.

One member suggested F.W. used the consultation process to `take over'. F.W., he said

> want to run it all. They swamp any meeting. However strong willed, R. and D.C. is always put upon by F.W..

As well as the use of numbers, another tactic which was, he suggested, used by F.W. managers was to `broaden the area of considerations so that it (a working party) never gets off the ground'. Consultation was seen as a way of losing control.

Speed of Decision Making

When it came to the speed of decision making, F.W. managers felt that they often had little or no time to respond to proposals initiated in R. and D.C. In the presence of R. and D.C. managers, one F.W. manager said

> we respect your drive to get things done, it's one feature you've sorted out.

He implied that his own team had not done so. In private, and at team meetings, reservations were expressed on a particular issue unrelated to expenditure reductions. One member said

> F.W. is not ready to go at the same pace;

another that

> F.W. needs to discuss items, but there's feeling that R. and D.C. are steaming ahead.

R. and D.C. were said to be showing

> an incredible lack of caution.

For F.W., time was important to

get it right now or live with the consequences for a long time.

A short time scale was

> a strategy that has been used before and I don't like it.

That is, time was deliberately restricted thereby reducing opportunities to oppose or make changes in proposals. Whilst F.W. recognised that consultation takes time, it was felt that the advantages gained were worth the delay. The R. and D.C. perspective on speed of action is reflected in the quotation above on consultation. That is, delay was less acceptable as

> some decisions require immediate action.

Speed of action was also important to

> reduce staff insecurity

according to the R. and D.C. team leader.

Significance of Formal Structure

The two groups also varied in the degree of significance they gave to formal structure. There was concern amongst F.W. managers that, to quote of one of their number, R. and D.C. were

> more interested in staffing and structure than care.

For F.W. managers the specification of the professional aspect of the work preceded decisions on structure. In general R. and D.C. managers were perceived to be more concerned with structure by their colleagues. Thus, a F.W. manager said:

In R. and D.C. the accent is on structure: formal authority not informal, assigned authority. Their reasons for action are directions from above.

Structure, and its creation, was significant for R. and D.C. managers because it reduced `the informal nature of work arrangements'. Structure was not seen to pre-empt professional decisions, but rather provide a foundation for them. Firstly, level of post and salary offered would determine the type of person applying for a post, and the qualifications or experience they would bring. In turn such recruits to the organisation would be able to participate in the formulation of professional objectives. Unsurprisingly, R. and D.C. members also felt that structural position was a significant determinant of managerial behaviour.

Essentially then the two management groups differed both about the significance of structure in determining managerial behaviour, and about what comes first in implementing change: task definition, or the creation of a structure within which the task is performed. They also differed in their views on consultation and speed of decision making.

Internal Variety

Managers were also aware of difference within their own groups, which would seem to militate against a claim to a common sub-culture.

A F.W. manager, in describing R. and D.C. management, provided an example of this apparent contradiction:

> It would never occur to me, or my colleagues to say this kind of thing, (my staff). It's paternalistic. It always makes me laugh when one member of F.W.M.T. uses `my' about his staff.

This member could therefore identify a difference within his own team yet still talked as if there were in fact none. In this instance it is perhaps a question of sample size: as only one member expresses an attitude which is out of line with the team perspective, it could be dismissed. The examination below of internal differences provides additional explanations of how they are managed.

The F.W. team leader was able to distinguish between formal or controlling, and informal or consultative, styles of management amongst F.W. managers. A F.W. manager described his own management style as

> formal, on a continuum with at one end an over controlled, formal style, and at the other a consensual, feelings style. I am near the former, but still somewhere near the centre. I believe in consultation but retain the right to decide. I'm paid to take responsibility.

He envied a F.W. colleague whose style was

> to derive managerial influence from deep emotional contact with the people under him.

Another F.W. manager said

> the basis of my style is close personal relations with people, and sharing. Other managers communicate in writing.

Another said his F.W. colleagues were suspicious of his management style, which was

> a co-operative model: everyone has an equal say and management is bound by the majority decision. In F.W. the commitment to open management hides a variety of styles.

Another manager defined F.W. style generally as

> participative, and democratic, with two exceptions; they pay lip service to the idea even if they don't practise it.

Another defined F.W.'s style as

> generally participative and consultative, though some members are into structure, elitism and hierarchy.

Reference to paying lip service, and commitment obscuring variety indicate the mechanisms whereby individual differences are suppressed in team meetings, thus enabling members to maintain their view of a collective attitude. An awareness of differences of approach did not lead to individuals who deviated being excluded from the group, nor change members' perceptions of their sub-culture, as long as these differences did not impinge on the group setting.

Another tactic which gave the appearance of a collective view was avoidance of issues which were known to be divisive. Thus one F.W. manager said that, in F.W.M.T. meetings,

> difficult issues are not raised because they would polarise the group.

The group's relationship with R. and D.C. for example was a `hidden problem, not discussed'. Some members laid the responsibility for this strategy with their team leader. Thus one member said the team leader

> was very denying in not taking issues up. He thinks there will be too many negatives around that area, he doesn't want to get into it. The real issues are not discussed, but old items are.

My observations, and comments from other members, suggest that responsibility for avoiding issues can be assigned to both team members and their leader. In the following chapter this matter is discussed in relation to expenditure reductions. What remains questionable is whether avoidance is a typical strategy to retain what Bennis (1969) terms `inward (and always fragile) harmony' (p. 29) of the group or a strategy peculiar to F.W.M.T. and thus an idiosyncratic aspect of their culture. An R. & D.C. manager suggested the same strategy was apparent in the R. & D.C. management team.

> People are not prepared to talk about their problems (in the team). They're more likely to be criticised than get a sympathetic hearing

Thus issues were avoided because of the known negative response they would generate. Avoidance then is a technique for maintaining harmony which is not peculiar to one sub-culture. In defining culture, Jaques (1951) refers to

> customary ways of thinking and doing which are shared to a
> greater or lesser degree by all its members (p. 257).

The above indicates the mechanisms whereby differences are suppressed in group settings, thus enabling the group to retain a collective view of itself. When `difficult issues' are raised, as in the case of F.W.M.T. and expenditure reductions, the sub-culture of the group is both exposed and reassessed, as we shall see in Chapter VI. `Cuts', said a F.W. manager

> highlighted rather than created divisions within the group

because members debated, rather than took for granted, what the right course of action was. New behaviours, such as competition, were observed which were not in line with the group's concept of itself.

Stringency was thus what Pettigrew (1979) termed a `critical event' because it exposed differences.

External Awareness

Members of each management team were aware of how they were characterised by members of other teams. Knowledge of sub-cultures was thus public rather than being confined to in-group members. For example, an R. and D.C. manager said

> F.W. feel Residential is managed with an iron hand. The
> typical managerial relationship is one of bureaucratic
> distance or dictatorship with no consultation or corporate
> way of working. F.W. keep hinting that I don't consult staff,
> and when I do, I dictate to them.

In private, members sometimes qualified the picture they presented in public of the other team's sub-culture by references to `generalisations' and `stereotypes'. For example, the R. and D.C. team leader said of F.W..

I try not to do so (stereotype) but do it all the time. F.W.
managers didn't want to lose their political virginity. They
didn't want to get their hands dirty by participating in the
management of reductions.

An R. and D.C. manager said

The generalised image R. and D.C. have of them (F.W.
managers) is long-haired political radicals who are out for all
they can get.

Awareness of internal group differences was also apparent from private
communications between managers, in which group members disassociated
themselves from their team's perspective. For example two members of
F.W.M.T. were said to have told an R. and D.C. manager that they were at
odds with their team's views on expenditure reductions. Two members of R.
and D.C.M.T. were said to privately disagree with their team's view of
F.W.M.T. and its relationship to R. and D.C.M.T. But knowledge of these
differences did not affect the way each group symbolised the other, because
they were not used to qualifying the generalised group image in team
meetings. There was a tendency instead either to generalise about a group's
values using the groups's response to particular issues, or to use experience
with one or two group members to generalise about the membership as a
whole. Team meetings provided a setting where this could be done. They
were used as a means of cultural elaboration and maintenance, though this
was not their official purpose.

The Significance of Team Meetings

Sub-cultures were maintained, and reinforced at team meetings through the
construction members placed on responses to routine or critical issues, and
on interactions with the other group. This analysis is developed below. The
process of collective behaviour also served this end except when difficult
issues were raised. Team meetings were a source of information on the

activities of non-members which provided, as a contrastive device, support for the group's self-image, and confirmed their view of the other group.

Both teams considered as a routine issue a recommendation for the adoption of a system of accelerated increments: outstanding members of staff could be moved more quickly than usual up the incremental scale. R. and D.C. managers adopted it with no discussion after the matter was presented by their leader to the group. F.W. managers on the other hand, discussed the same matter at length in terms of numbers involved, time limits, why the system was being reinstated, the unions views and the process involved. They were informed that

> R. and D.C. has recommended two or three people.

Finally they decided not to implement the system. Process differences between the two groups will be considered later in this chapter. What is examined here is the grounds for this rejection, or how the proposal was constructed as being unacceptable.

In discussing the problem, one F.W. manager said the procedure was

> an invidious method of promotion.

Another said

> Social Services are the only Department where this system is seen as objectionable. Other Departments are authoritarian, hierarchical and accept patronage.

By rejecting the procedure, they rejected the values on which it was assumed to be based. They allied themselves with opposite values which were in line with the group's self-image. At the same time, unacceptable values were used to justify action, that is, why they were not prepared to operate the procedure.

In contrast, managers who operated the procedure, in this case R. and D.C., did so in support of values which were `objectionable' to F.W. managers. That R. and D.C. managers subscribed to such values was consistent with F.W.M.T.'s view of their R. and D.C. colleagues.

In referring to the critical issue of expenditure reductions the self image of R. and D.C. managers, and their image of F.W. managers, was reinforced at a team meeting by their leader. Whilst not an agenda item, he made a long speech of which the following is an extract:

> I feel there's a value difference between the two groups polarised by the cuts issue. There's a clear philosophical difference. F.W. say management responsibility for the cuts is not theirs, and then oppose them. But area officers are managers. R. and D.C. accept cuts and thereby keep control over what is done. I think that's a tenable position. R. and D.C. put forward a legitimate claim: F.W. closed an area office.

This interpretation of events involved structural position (being a manager) as a determinant of action, and value differences as the basis for different responses. It was accepted without question and is an example of what Pettigrew (1979) terms the process of symbolism. Both he and Geertz (1975) have pointed to the importance of this process in the creation and maintenance of culture. For Pettigrew symbol construction is the process whereby

> a group represents its situation to itself and to the outside world where it emphasises, distorts and ignores (p. 574).

As well as representing its situation to itself, this speech also represented the activities of a group of non-members, and contrasted the two. During interviews R. and D.C. managers provided a far more detailed picture of F.W. activities than is represented by the above description, yet this version of events at a less specific level of symbolisation was acceptable to the group.

An example of interaction between groups was provided when F.W. representatives were involved in consultation with R. and D.C. One gave the following account to the F.W.M.T. of this:

> The jargon and way of doing things is so different, it's incomprehensible. Papers are circulated too late, using the language of function and matrix, a very boring systems analysis. There's no discussion of whether this is the best way of doing it, its double-Dutch. Take the way they arrive at their decisions and settle them. If someone says we need five staff, and someone else three, they'll settle for four. Its a

numbers game. The moment I put in a F.W. perspective, I was shouted down. When I said it (the proposed span of supervision) would be out of the question in F.W., I was told it was not the same (in Residential). We've got to the state of believing the meetings are held for our benefit and the work goes on in other forums. They want a geographically based area structure, but don't know what it is. They use the same jargon as F.W., but I've discovered it has different meanings. Supervision means washing hair (of client) not sitting and talking to staff about the job.

The following analysis focuses on the content of this account as a means of maintaining the sub-culture of the F.W.M.T. The account supports rather than challenges the group's typification of itself as having a common perspective on management issues such as span and definition of supervision. It also describes methods of analysis and decision making to which the F.W. group would not subscribe. Differences are so great that terms such as `incomprehensible' and `double-Dutch' are appropriate.

F.W. managers listened to the description with sympathetic understanding, indicating that what was described was not a unique or unexpected experience. The group's taken for granted view of R. and D.C. managers, their methods of analysis and decision making, was not challenged. Just as an alternative `F.W. perspective' was `shouted down' in the forum being described, so in the F.W.M.T. there was no suggestion that the decision making method described was anything other than misconceived, nor that F.W. managers should consider amending their own methods of decision making in the light of the alternative approach described.

Working together, sharing superordinate goals such as client allocation decisions, does not necessarily overcome differences, as authors such as the Sherifs (1953) suggest. In this instance, it had quite the reverse effect; it served to highlight group differences.

Differentiating Team Processes

Whilst both middle management teams had the traditional accoutrements of formal meetings, such as agendas, papers and minutes, and had a pre-defined group of individuals who attended, the manner in which the task of collective decision making was managed was significantly different. These differences provided data which supported the perception of R. and D.C.M.T. as action orientated, and F.W.M.T. as discussion orientated.

Each meeting comprised the middle managers in each respective division, their team leader and a representative from the administrative division. The R. and D.C. group comprised nine members, and the F.W. team fifteen. On regular occasions a staff representative attended F.W.M.T.; no staff representative attended R. and D.C.M.T. F.W. managers thus acknowledged the relevance of staff to their deliberations; occasionally the representative made a contribution, or presented the views of staff. Such an acknowledgement was not observed in R. and D.C.M.T..

R. and D.C.M.T. meetings were less frequent than F.W.M.T. meetings. In March and April R. and D.C.M.T. met twice, whereas F.W.M.T. met on five occasions. Usually R. and D.C.M.T. meetings lasted for up to two hours; F.W. meetings took between three and four hours. R. and D.C covered a larger number of agenda items in the time and on two occasions they dealt with eleven topics. The largest number of items considered by F.W.M.T. was four; three items was more usual, and on two occasions they considered only one. R. and D.C.M.T. invariably dealt with all items on the agenda whereas F.W.M.T. did not; their leader said it was difficult to reach the end of agendas.

R. and D.C. meetings were firmly directed by their team leader. He likened his role to `the conductor of an orchestra' Members agreed that their meetings were directed:

> Peter (the team leader) usually tells us what to do, as you must have noticed ... Meetings are used in a fairly directive way.

Another manager said that there was

> less open discussion than in F.W.M.T. The group works in a physical sense, it works through long agendas, compared

with the agendas of F.W.M.T. We come to decisions, and don't have meetings unless there's a full agenda. I've been to a few F.W. meetings, with very erudite discussions on the social work task. They come across as wordy and indecisive. In R. and D.C. we move forward.

A F.W. manager said when describing the two management teams

R. and D.C. deal with day to day issues, with details and specifics. R. and D.C. is practical: F.W. theoretical.

Thus in terms of the amount of consideration given to each issue, and the type of consideration, theoretical or practical, the teams were seen to differ.

Though the team leader felt `R. and D.C.M.T. works as a group' and said he `was trying to hand over to them', that is, become less directive, I did not observe this, and neither did other members. Some felt, to quote one of their number, that whilst the group managers worked at an

administrative management level, it offers no support emotionally.

The meeting was seen to serve

Peter's (the team leader's) needs.

Another manager referred to lack of trust. Though not all members were happy with the way their team operated this was not raised at meetings. This is a further example of the strategy of avoidance which was referred to earlier in the chapter. However, there was agreement on how meetings operated, that is, in a directed manner.

F.W.M.T. meetings were not directed by their leader. He described his style as `very non-directive' as he was `finding his feet' and as a new member was feeling his way. In his view `F.W.M.T. meetings ramble'. Members of the group agreed with this, and my observations supported this view. One member said that the meetings produced

few decisions. They are floundering, unsure of where their focus is.

The meetings were characterised by another member as

> rambling with off-centre topics which are not immediately relevant.

Another remarked that there are

> few decisions: items come and go, with no decisions.

One member explained this as follows:

> F.W.M.T. works at a high level of theory. Its broad theoretical approach, with few decisions, may be quite right sometimes, except when the specific task is to make up its mind. Because of the way it's functioned in the past, this is not possible.

In this instance, the group's traditional style was seen as inhibiting decision-making.

An alternative explanation was to blame the team leader. For example, one manager said

> John (the team leader) is less directive and likes informal leadership. He's pleased if someone else takes a lead.

Other managers described him as `weak' and `out of his depth' and referred to `lack of direction from the team leader'. Thus there were two explanations of the group's indecisiveness: traditional pattern of behaviour, or leadership. In view of members' preference for participative management, and the fact that `direction' in R. and D.C. was seen as reprehensible, it is possible that the leadership style explanation is an example of transference or scape-goating: the group's deficiencies were loaded on to one member, their new leader. In addition, the introduction of a difficult issue, expenditure reductions, did not facilitate the group's process as it required the group to adopt a new approach rather than continue with a traditional one. If the difficult issue was to be dealt with effectively, a move from a `broad theoretical approach' to taking action was necessary.

An example of this broad theoretical approach is provided by the group's consideration, reported above, of accelerated increments. In F.W.M.T. there was an expressed need to agree on criteria for selection, which was absent in R. and D.C.M.T. F.W. managers expressed concern about the effects of the procedure on their relations with staff, and rejected the values on which the procedure was seen to be based. For R. and D.C. managers neither of these were an issue. F.W. managers decided not to take action to implement the procedure, whereas R. and D.C. managers did. In one group there was in-depth consideration of the matter leading to a decision not to implement; in the other the reverse.

The Functions of Sub-Culture

Sub-culture was used both as a descriptive and as an analytical device to give order to the activities of groups. It enabled them to describe themselves, both internally and to outsiders. They could also describe outsiders, using dimensions on which there was some degree of collective agreement. It provided an orientation to management role performance in two ways. The activities of the group were facilitated by a `taken for granted' collective perspective, thus enabling the group to function in general terms rather than reconsidering how they would manage an issue on each occasion they met. Additionally new issues were made sense of, using the `taken for granted' set of values of the group, rather than accepting definitions provided by other sources. Sub-culture was used to explain and justify behaviour, by reference to group values and previous behavioural patterns. That is, action was explained and justified as being in tune with the group's collective view of themselves, and the type of action they would typically take. It also involved notions of right and wrong, and enabled members to evaluate what they saw going on around them. It provided an orientation to events rather than a fully explicated and binding set of responses. Members could choose whether or not to act in terms of their group's culture in group settings. However if they did not, these unsanctioned actions, and the values underlying them, would become the subject for debate.

D.M.T. Sub-Culture

The D.M.T. is now examined in terms of the sub-culture of that group as perceived by members and as observed by the researcher. Group members invariably referred to the team leader (the Director) being the major factor in determining how the group operated: it operated in particular ways because of his personal needs, and because he chose to focus on short term rather than long term issues. The team shared with R. and D.C. managers a structural construction of managerial behaviour and values, and a preoccupation with day to day issues. Like F.W.M.T., it was seen to have a lack of purpose, particularly in the field of long-term planning. The Director exerted strong control by inhibiting the group from becoming an effective decision-making unit, both in the way he chaired the meeting, and in the topics that he introduced.

The culture of the D.M.T. reflected and met the Director's need to retain control both of the meeting itself, and of the issues involved. I was told by a member that

> The Director is not into management by consensus. He says that at the end of the day the decisions are up to him.

Another said

> He prefers dealing with individuals one by one; not at meetings because he can manipulate the former. Meetings are threatening to him.

Thus collective decision making was threatening because the head of the organisation could not retain control over either decisions or individuals. An example of this control was given by a relatively new member: He said

> when I first started the Director announced items at the meeting. Having agendas in advance was unheard of until recently.

A similar point was made by another member:

we need to have agendas and discussion papers circulated before the meeting. Too often the D.M.T. doesn't get information in time and one cannot contribute fully to a discussion.

Restricting the amount of time members have to consider an issue reduces their ability to contribute.

In the Director's opinion

the team works very well,

but other members disagreed in private; no-one however raised this matter in the group setting. The function of team meetings, the Director said

was obvious to a certain extent, though this is easier said than done.

He saw its purpose as twofold: creating a team spirit to present a united front to outsiders; and developing departmental policy. It did not in fact fulfil its second function because

it's inevitable we consider other matters, nuts and bolts issues not policy matters. Often items need a quick decision. At the moment it works very well even if many matters are irrelevant to social services; sometimes they're totally irrelevant.

Whatever the reason, the Director clearly set more store by considering nuts and bolts issues, even irrelevant ones, than policy matters.

Other members referred to a

lack of interest in long-term planning.

The meeting was

often concerned with short-term decisions and cannot consider long-term policy implications.

One member expressed a preference for

corporate planning: that's the way I'd like to see it going; it's impossible and impractical that it doesn't happen. I'm often unsure of what the meeting's (D.M.T.) purpose is; for example, the discussion of the use of portakabins. Often we get bogged down in detail. We don't discuss general policy matters, which we should do.

Another said

the Department's like a ship which works well, but has no set course, it goes where the wind blows it. The D.M.T. discuss whether to give the sailors a tot of rum on Christmas Day. The D.M.T. is criticised in the Department for never reaching a decision:

that is, the D.M.T. is concerned with minor issues, whilst ignoring the major ones, especially that of providing the Department with direction.

Lack of interest in Departmental strategy or long-term plans was laid at the Director's door. Thus one member said the leader was

old, tired and had seen it all before. He's not interested in forward planning as he's convinced there will be no change in the end.

Another said the Director

prefers to put things off - he believes problems will go away or a solution will be found; sometimes this works. He's responsive not directive. He doesn't go out of his way to look for problem areas; he gives few initiatives. He feels the Department's running O.K..

Another said the Department's senior management was like

a doughnut with nothing in the middle.

There was

lack of guidance and direction from the centre.

This lack of guidance and direction was on occasions linked to the Director's management of the political interface: thus one senior manager said

> the Director won't make a decision until he knows how members (councillors) feel.

The Director himself referred to `political nous', that is, knowing when to introduce an item to politicians, what the current political climate was and how this would influence its acceptability. A team member said the Director was

> a good political survivor; always at the back of his mind is what the political reaction will be. He's not like some chief officers who pride themselves on going against members.

The Director said he would not put an item up to politicians unless he knew that the response would be positive because

> it's useless to fly in the face of resistance.

He then qualified this by referring to

> situations where you have to have on record you've drawn the matter to members attention even if they don't proceed with it.

The Director's focus then was external, towards politicians, rather than internal, towards providing direction and formulating long-term plans. Lack of such plans facilitated the former focus by allowing the Director room to manoeuvre in the fluid environment of the political system.

In addition to considering irrelevant and minor items the Director maintained control by disrupting the process of team meetings. One member said

> meetings are badly organised, discussions ramble on for too long. The D.M.T. doesn't like making decisions.

The Director was said by another member to be

> not a strong chairman; he lets people ramble.

My impressions, as an observer, supported this view. I also noted a number of strategies used by the Director to disrupt meetings: physical withdrawal by leaving the room; inability to deal with discussion papers conveyed by remarks such as

> `which paper are we on?', `I've not seen that';

and apologetic interventions such as

> `I'm not trying to be difficult but...', `I don't want to complicate matters but...', and `I don't want to make a meal of this, I am just genuinely asking'.

One member suggested that it suited the Director's purpose to let people ramble because

> they don't reach a decision. After a time people are exhausted and will agree to anything.

Thus undirected discussions prevented decision making, or enabled the Director to impose his will indirectly by a process of attrition. Another member suggested the Director was looking for dialogue:

> He's not verbally articulate and uses things others have said. I've heard phrases I've used when he's been arguing the same case.

From my observations the Director certainly did not appear particularly comfortable in D.M.T. meetings. But a dysfunctional process is functional if it serves someone's purposes, in this case, the Director's. Thus on items where he did not know the political response, the process introduced delay, and the Director retained the ultimate power of decision making. On items which would be put to politicians, rambling discussions provided a rehearsal for the type of discussion he might expect to have with councillors.

The culture of this group involved decision postponement with a focus on short-term matters, and an avoidance of long-term, strategic issues, using a process of confusion whereby the Director maintained control.

Summary

As a means of understanding differing managerial responses to the management of stringency, the dimension of management group sub-culture was introduced. This dimension both reflects members' explanations, and broadens the area of enquiry from one confined either to characteristics of the reductions themselves, or to issues of financial management. The data suggests that there was a strong awareness of management group culture, though the term `culture' was used very infrequently. There was an expressed awareness of management groups holding certain values in common, and behaving in certain distinguishable ways. Thus F.W. managers saw themselves as valuing consultation and participation in performing their management tasks. Conversely, R. and D.C. managers described themselves as `benign despots' and were described as directive. The D.M.T. was seen to be directed by its leader, but did not provide strategic direction to middle managers because it did not value long-term planning.

It seems that, as well as an explanatory and descriptive device, the dimension of sub-culture provides a guide to action and attitudes. This guide includes evaluations of right and wrong. Though sub-culture was not totally deterministic, in that members could choose whether or not to act in support of their group's taken for granted assumptions, it nevertheless provided a significant device for understanding different managerial responses to decline. These responses are considered in the following chapter.

5 Managerial responses to expenditure reductions

Introduction

This chapter explores the plurality of managerial responses to expenditure reductions and their justifications. References to rationality and defensive reaction in the literature on decline management are examined in the light of the data. Responses of avoidance, co-operation, overt resistance and withdrawal are described. Thus the differing responses and rationalities of the D.M.T., R. and D.C.M.T. and F.W.M.T. are identified and considered below.

Two analytical frameworks utilise the concept of rationality to describe and analyse managers' responses to stringency. One, as was seen in Chapter 3, focuses on movement from the political to the rational, or an increase in rationality. Decision making becomes based to a greater extent on analytical and budgetary procedures which take account of demand, expenditure and policy. Greenwood et al (1980) identify this response, which is a major tenet of organisational monetarism.

Political and rational are categories used by Jick and Murray (1982). Following Levine (1978), they analyse decline by contrasting the `political' and `rational', both as sources of decline, and as categories of response strategies that managers adopt. `Rational' decline stems from an

> appraisal of costs and benefits, efficiency and effectiveness (p. 147),

on the part of the funding source. With `political' decline, that source aims

> to protect or increase its power or status, or respond to the irrational whim of more powerful others (p. 147).

`Rational' responses, which are similar to those suggested by Greenwood et al above (1980), result from `rational' decline; `political' responses, such as making reductions which cause the most pressure, stem from `political' decline. Whilst the authors are rightly concerned with members' subjective interpretation, their categories do not represent the variety of rationalities evident in my data. Nor does their causal linkage between source and response account for different responses to the same source of decline.

The alternative framework suggests the antithesis between `political' and `rational' is unhelpful (Self: 1980; Wright: 1980). Instead, a multiplicity of competing rationalities operate in decline (Glennester: 1980). That a variety of rationalities operate in any social setting is argued by a number of authors. Weber (1968) points to a number of rationalities, termed substantive, that can be used in addition to that of formal rationality. Garfinkel (1975) identifies fourteen different types. Eldridge (1968), and Martin and Fryer (1970), refer to different rationalities in use during redundancy management. Jick and Murray (1982), stress the importance of members' interpretation in determining responses to reductions. Rose (1980), and Schick (1980), support this approach. Schick states

> Scarcity is both a matter of attitude and circumstances (p. 114).

It is, he says, determined by perceptions, not according to some objective standards. Rose (1980), refers to the

> multiple meaning of the cuts (p. 204).

Glennester (1980), presents a stimulating hypothesis by identifying four competing rationalities which operate with expenditure reductions: strategic, political, professional and consumer. Strategic rationality has the same meaning as `rationality' in Greenwood et al (1980). For Glennester, rationality means action which is logical to a group in pursuit of its own interests.

By applying this model within an organisation, the hypothesis is confirmed and elaborated as follows. Firstly bureaucratic and administrative rationalities are isolated from professional rationality, whereas Glennester deals with the three together. Secondly, a particular rationality is not identified only with a particular group. Managers can, for example, act in terms of political rationality. Thirdly, management groups can behave in terms of a number of different rationalities: there are competing rationalities within, as well as between, groups. Glennester implies that a role group only acts in terms of its own rationality. Fourthly, rationalities additional to those of Glennester are identified. The definition used here of rationality as `logics for action' is wider than that of Glennester, in that it includes the values (Weber: 1968) as well as the interests of group members. It is based on members' accounts of their strategies for action and their reasons, or justifications.

Writing about defensive reactions, Bion (1961) divides defense mechanisms in groups into fight and flight: with fight, there is a move towards the source of conflict; with flight a move away. Fink et al (1971) regard defensive retreat as the response to crisis, which follows initial `shock' or panic and disorganisation. Defensive retreat involves an attempt to maintain the status quo to avoid reality and change. Defensive retreat of flight is thus an initial coping strategy. In the absence of planning, Hirschhorn (1983: a) sees fight or flight as the only response available to managers. Both of these were observed responses to expenditure reductions in the organisation studied.

Director's Management Team

The team produced its recommendations for reductions by a process which did not accord with strategic rationality, but rather with administrative and bureaucratic rationality. There was an absence of long-term plans in respect of demand, policy, and expenditure. Decisions were taken in the light of recommendations received, papers produced by the non-executive member responsible for finance and as one team member put it, on the basis of

gut level, hearsay evidence.

One senior manager described the D.M.T.'s recommendations for reductions as follows:

the cake was sliced horizontally not vertically.

Limited resources were taken from a number of work areas, rather than one area being totally removed. Levine (1978 and 1979), terms this decrementalism, and Glassberg (1978) calls it incremental decreases, that is, using and preserving current budget heads as a framework for determining reductions. Most literature on budget reductions focuses on this method, which Glassberg suggests will reduce the likelihood of innovation because it restricts decision making to existing categories. This method is also referred to as the `efficiency option' (Gill and Pratt: 1986; Whetton: 1981).

Spending was reduced by introducing what was termed a `managed vacancy element': posts were kept vacant to save money. This is an example of administrative rationality. In effect the decision as to what services to withhold was passed down the organisational hierarchy to those who had the responsibility for managing the client contact level of service delivery. In theory, they could decide whether or not to reallocate all, or part of, the workload of posts which became vacant.

This was the interpretation placed on the D.M.T.'s strategy by F.W.M.T. members. It was indeed the intention as confirmed in a document which the F.W.M.T. leader presented to his team. This document, which had been approved by D.M.T., was the only detailed written statement which addressed the issue of managing reductions produced by any organisational manager. It contained the following point of principle:

I do not believe that it is possible to detail to any great extent the priorities that should be adopted across the division. In order to maintain flexibility these decisions should be made as close to the situation as possible.

Only two priorities were referred to subsequently in the paper: keeping spending within the budget, and protecting services to clients. The latter was distinguished from other activities, such as working parties, which did `not impinge on service delivery'.

This strategy broadly accords with Glennester's view (1980) that:

> it makes sense for administrators simply to squeeze the budgets and staffing complements that professional workers have available to them and let them do the rationing. (p. 377).

Such administrative rationality, or in layman's language `passing the buck', where the provision of some services is dependent on factors such as employees finding other jobs, or not, is the antithesis of strategic rationality.

Team members operated in terms of bureaucratic rationality by unquestioningly accepting and following instructions from above. As one senior manager put it:

> Officers can voice their professional opinions but ultimately they have to carry out Council policy. Officers should work within the guidelines set down by members.

A distinction is drawn here between `professional opinions' and `carrying out orders', the latter being given pre-eminence. This distinction and the significance accorded to each of the two categories, points up the nature of bureaucratic rationality. There was no evidence that team members questioned their instructions, or even contemplated doing so. As the director said:

> It's best to manage with what we have.

They got on with the job, within councillors' guidelines.

Whilst some team members argued for strategic rationality in the form of planning and prioritising, the Director questioned the extent to which this was necessary, could be effective, or was within the team's task domain. The matter was not pursued.

The team used two priorities in their discussions of expenditure reduction recommendations. The first was termed `members idiosyncrasies', that is, councillors' preferences. Councillors, said senior managers, were

obsessed with certain areas

which could not

be touched.... You accept this as part of the work in local government.

There was no suggestion that this priority arose at a time of reductions nor that it was any less important then, but rather that it was a constant feature of `work in local government'. The second priority was described by a member as

protecting R. and D.C. from the worst effects of the cuts.

This priority was justified as follows:

F.W. received a larger share of the cake in the past, so it's only fair that they should have a higher percentage cut.

Reference was also made to Council policy, agreed prior to reductions, to upgrade R. and D.C. by providing more resources for that division. Thus a priority was justified in terms of past resource allocation patterns and Council policy, rather than in terms of a department-wide strategy. It resulted in one division being protected (R. and D.C.) at the expense of another (F.W.).

Within these parameters various steps were taken to increase revenue by, for example, instituting charges for services such as home-helps. A review of high-spending areas, such as transport, was instituted but progress was slow. The D.M.T. thus aimed to deal with resource reductions by increasing income from other sources, and by a scrutiny of high spending areas of work.

A research proposal which would, it was claimed, put the team's strategic decision making on some sort of `rational' basis was rejected. Interestingly, the focus of the research was managers' values in relation to the various services provided by the organisation, and data would be generated to rank those services into a hierarchy of priorities. In contrast it was suggested by the Director, during the discussion of this issue, that priority for service delivery should be on a `first come, first serve' basis, that is, a `chronological basis'. Whilst the research proposal related to services, the latter concerned a prioritisation of clients on a chronological basis.

The argument for some form of strategic rationality was based on members' recent experience, which they constructed as being less than ideal. The expressed need, both privately, and in the forum of team meetings, was for prioritisation and planning.

The absence of any preparation for reduction was noted. One member said

> It was known in January/February that there would be an expenditure review. Why didn't the Department take action then?.

He went on to say that

> long term planning is a management job. One needs to be able to relate to something planned. They (councillors) may not stick to it, and we will have to accommodate this. In the past Social Services grew by grabbing money from the pot as it came up, which was appropriate, but now, with no money we need formal planning.

Another member said

> I'm going to get the D.M.T. to prioritise as a priority.

The reductions exercise had been

> fraught with prejudice, and based on gut level, hearsay evidence. The Department cannot go through it again.

What was needed was

> formalised procedures to assist the Department in its long term aims by formulating clearer criteria for decisions It

would be wrong ...to pretend there were no reductions and no effects.

Another member said that a serious consideration of expenditure reductions should have involved a

realistic assessment of priorities.

Long-term planning, criteria setting and prioritisation were seen as necessary to manage reductions, and by some of its members to be the responsibility of the team. They might not be acceptable to councillors but that was no reason for inaction. Finally it was `wrong' to deny the reduced circumstances and their effect on organisational members.

Long-term planning and criteria setting was rejected by the team leader on a number of grounds. He said:

Things are not as bad as they're made out ...there's still money round the margins. It's a question of how to move money from A to B,

that is, from one budget head to another. He believed

members (councillors) should establish priorities. Our attempts are useless: it's a political decision at the end of the day.

He dismissed `sophisticated criteria setting used in other authorities' as less than useful as

their (councillors) highest priority might be our lowest one, because of the different priorities of staff and council. We're at the mercy of members.

Councillors would

not stick their necks out,

they preferred

leaving decisions until the last minute.

These were often taken on the grounds of `political expediency' rather than on the basis of what was best for the service. This was especially true of reductions which were a `political' issue where councillors could not agree amongst themselves.

He thus minimised or denied the seriousness of the Department's financial situation, assigned the job of prioritising to councillors, denied that the D.M.T. had any power, and pointed up an opposition between long-term planning, and the decision making process of politicians. Yet he was happy for the job of prioritising to be assigned to middle managers, as noted above. What emerges from this is that he did not see the task to be that of the D.M.T., and wished to avoid it.

He took this position even though he predicted that

things (financial stringency) will get worse,

and despite recognising that reductions

drove staff to distraction.

He said staff

needed help and talking through

the experience. There was however no evidence that this was put into practice, despite the F.W.M.T. team requesting guidance from the D.M.T. on a number of occasions. For example, minutes of a F.W.M.T. meeting record:

concern was expressed that little or no guidance had been given to (team) members on how these cuts should be achieved. It was therefore agreed to urge the D.M.T. to issue guidelines.

Thus even where there is both internal and external pressure on a senior management team to adopt some form of strategic rationality, such pressure can be, and is, resisted if those in control see no benefit in the adoption of such an approach. There is no automatic adoption of strategic rationality in response to expenditure reductions, as the concept of organisational monetarism predicts. In fact, as we saw in Chapter 4, long-term strategic planning was not regarded by members as being an aspect of the D.M.T.'s group culture. This suggests that a group's culture, that is, the constructs whereby they attach meaning, will be of great significance in determining responses to expenditure reductions. The connection between group culture and managerial responses to expenditure reductions is further explored in Chapters 6 and 8.

The D.M.T. was in a position of some uncertainty, both in terms of knowing how much was to be reduced, and what councillors would accept, because the latter changed their minds. For example, increased charges for some services were initially unacceptable but later became acceptable. This uncertainty was exacerbated by another aspect of the group's culture; it did not put items up to politicians unless they knew there would be a positive response. No attempt was made however to reduce this uncertainty by instituting some form of strategic planning, and the guidance offered to middle managers when expenditure was being reviewed was very broad.

It follows from the above that services were not prioritised. F.W.M.T. minutes record that the following points were made in relation to the preparation of reduction recommendations: no more overspending; all spending areas, not just the F.W., were open to their scrutiny; there should be no `sacred cows', that is, automatically protected areas; reductions should have the minimum effect on service; priority should be given to life-supporting, rather than life-enhancing, services.

Though the last point may appear a priority, the distinction was not referred to in D.M.T. discussions. It was not put to R. & D.C.M.T. nor was it accepted by F.W.M.T.. In fact the D.M.T. did not consider that they had provided any priorities of service.

R. & D.C.M.T. was told, according to one of their members to

make cutbacks that could be best absorbed by the service

and

to consider major policy changes such as closing homes; minor items which added together would produce a large amount; and reduction options for other divisions.

Both sets of instructions can be seen to widen the area each group considered, by the invitation to consider divisions other than their own, and in F.W.M.T.'s case, the inclusion of `sacred cows'. They assume a detailed knowledge of departmental activities, skill in budgeting, a willingness to participate, and a willingness to reduce previously protected areas. The extent to which these assumptions were correct is apparent from data presented below.

The only guidance on managing the effects of reductions was the document referred to above for the F.W.M.T.. Essentially, it proposed an administrative system, but was vague on purposes. In particular it suggested the creation of a panel of F.W. managers who would decide which, if any, of the managed vacancies (posts left vacant to save money) should be filled. There was, however, no guidance on the basis for these decisions. The pattern of recommendations that emerged from the document is generally in line with the observations and predictions of works on response to crisis and decline, such as Hamblin (1958), Cazalis (1979) and Woods (1980): centralisation, more monitoring, more information, and greater scrutiny. For example the document recommended that

> up-to-date information about commitments and consequent financial forecasts should be available on a monthly basis.

There should be

> central oversight of budget heads ... all requests for agency placements should therefore come to the A.D. (team leader) or manager in charge who will have oversight of the whole (financial) situation, and who will give approval or not depending on the situation at the time.

The principal recommendation contained in the document concerned controls on, and monitoring of, spending, together with an administrative procedure for choosing which vacancies to fill. Prioritisation of services was left open, and was not made the subject of greater control. This suggests that studies which predict or recommend greater control as a response to reductions could usefully be qualified by reference to those areas where control is introduced or increased, and those areas where it is not.

101

Finally the D.M.T. had no strategy for dealing with non-co-operation. In response to F.W.M.T.'s refusal to recommend reductions in the `correct' way, D.M.T. did it for them, and criticised F.W.M.T.'s activities. F.W.'s opposition was dealt with initially by filling two F.W. posts which became the focus of resistance through industrial action. Subsequently, when the question of resistance was raised, the possibility of disciplinary action was mentioned, but senior managers were unsure what they could

legitimately ask staff to do.

The Director pointed out that

other divisions are managing, so should F.W.. They should at least try.

This was also the view of the D.M.T. Thus both middle management teams were seen to be operating in similar circumstances except that F.W.M.T. was regarded as just not trying. In fact it was apparent from what was said to me that some senior managers were aware of differences, but these were denied in public, as became clear from the intervention analysed in Chapter 7.

The D.M.T. operated in terms of administrative and bureaucratic rationality, and rejected strategic rationality, through a process of denial or defensive retreat. This applied to the seriousness of the financial situation; their influence with councillors; their responsibility for prioritising; and the different circumstances their middle management teams. They avoided long-term planning despite being in agreement that,as one member put it, reductions would be

around for some time.

Residential and Day Care Management Team

This team was perceived by non-members, and saw itself, as having co-operated in the expenditure reductions process: they accepted, or did not question, the need for reductions and their own role in the process. They came up with the required amounts on request and accepted the outcomes, according to members' accounts. The group operated in terms of bureaucratic rationality by following orders. They did this in terms of political rationality by recommending some unacceptable reductions, and in terms of professional rationality by expressing a concern for service protection. They also briefly adopted a fight strategy in relation to the F.W.M.T.

A member of R. and D.C.M.T. pointed out that

we don't like the cuts but do it anyway.

All of them believed it was their job to participate. This response was defined by one member as

the classic local government approach: follow instructions and don't get involved in the issue.

That is, 'following instructions' was the significant factor in determining action; 'the issue' to which the orders related was not.

The budgetary strategy adopted was a mixture of decrementalism and zero-based budgeting,that is, a consideration of base spending in particular areas. The latter strategy was used primarily 'for effect' rather than with any expectation that action would be taken. Two examples of this strategy were reported which paradoxically involved 'offering up' unacceptable reductions. The first was in fact termed 'unacceptable reductions' and the second 'making a case'. Glennester (1980) refers to this strategy as 'sore thumbs' (p. 372): offering up projects that would cause most political embarrassment, as an example of political rationality. In this instance though, and in contrast to Glennester's example, the strategists were administrators not politicians. They took action in terms of political rationality to obtain or retain resources, rather than in pursuit of a party political goal.

Unacceptable reductions involved offering up items 'for effect' as one member put it, in the certain knowledge that finance for the area concerned would not be reduced. For example, one R. and D.C. manager said

I suggested closing Prestwick House (an old people's home).
I knew they never would - they wouldn't touch the elderly.

Another said

> I was asked to prioritise, which I did, from shutting my
> section down to various other options. I knew members
> (councillors) wouldn't close me down, because I deal with
> the elderly. Our socialist employers have a weak spot for the
> elderly.

Another R. and D.C. manager said

> Our concern was to prepare our case.

This manager recommended a reduction - closing a children's home - then

> built up a case to make it impossible to do so. I got case
> histories of clients, referring to them being settled in schools
> and the cost of movement.

That is, he detailed the effect on clients of closure. As a result

> There was no way that home could close.

Thus a recommendation to save money by closure was qualified by
information which was seen to make the recommended act impossible.

Professional rationality, or a concern with determining what services
should be protected, was evident by members' attempts to retain control over
what areas were reduced, and what were preserved. The above is an example
of this: closing a children's home was unacceptable in professional terms, and
this was made apparent by supplying professional, as well as financial,
information on costs. In effect

> If we don't make the decisions, someone else will

said one manager, and so participating was seen as a way of exerting some
control over the decision making process. The direction of this control was
signified by this member, who described his strategy as follows

> offer up something as one way to protect the rest: cut non-
> essentials like garden maintenance.

104

What was thus protected were service areas which were considered essential, not in political, but in professional terms.

The group also recommended reductions in F.W. division which was perceived as a fight strategy and was explained by an R. and D.C. manager as follows: at an interdivisional management meeting on reductions

> R. and D.C. were made to look like lemons, with no opinions; we said nothing.

F.W. dominated the meeting and suggested closing a home and other cuts in R. & D.C..

> We felt under attack and decided to hit back.

This was based on two reactions:

> If they do it to us, we'll do it to them - its not very adult but,

and

> we do it or get shafted.

Additionally there was some irritation with F.W. managers because they were disinclined to reduce expenditure in their own division. As an R. and D.C. manager interpreted it

> it's OK to cut us, but not them, they're so important.

This F.W. `attack' was seen to `promote a corporate style' in R. and D.C.M.T., which was usually absent. At a second meeting with F.W. managers' `each R. and D.C. manager took a subject and spoke to it'. They came up with and presented `a list of cuts in F.W.'. At the same time F.W. management strategies were criticised by R. and D.C. managers; one member for example said that

> as council managers we should act in a management way.

R. and D.C. managers used this meeting to reinforce a construction of their strategies in relation to reductions as co-operative, to defend bureaucratic rationality or `acting as managers', and to attack F.W.'s resources and their rationalities.

The management of reduction outcomes was unproblematic for most members of the R. and D.C.M.T. The principle reason given was that their financial position had not been much affected.

I've come out well from the cuts

was how one R. and D.C. manager summarised his position. This represented the view of the majority of R. and D.C.M.T. members. Whilst one member said

any idiot can see I've fewer resources than last year,

few management problems associated with this loss were identified.

Thus R. and D.C. managers responded to reductions in terms of bureaucratic, political and professional rationalities, and utilised a fight strategy reactively and as a protective measure. The co-operative response of this team reflects aspects of the group's sub-culture, identified in the previous chapter, such as orientation towards action, and a willingness to follow orders.

Field Work Management Team

The F.W.M.T. presented themselves, and were perceived by non-team members, as adopting a strategy of resistance to expenditure reductions. The majority of F.W. managers rejected some of the rationalities presented previously in this chapter, in that they did not pass reduction decisions further down the hierarchy (administrative), they did not generally follow orders (bureaucratic) and they rejected a planning role (strategic). Instead they based their rationalities on professional, ideological, and political grounds, taking account of task definition and industrial relations. Their defensive responses of resistance and withdrawal were justified on these grounds.

Differences of opinion on strategy within the F.W.M.T. ranged from total opposition to co-operation;

I'm totally opposed to the cuts;

I'm nearer R. and D.C. on this: try to influence and manage cuts.

The latter, though, represented a minority view and some members were unsure; one manager for example said

I find it difficult. Politically and philosophically I'm opposed to the cuts but the reality is there's less money.

Another said

on cuts, I feel confused and torn. If I say no, I won't participate on cuts decisions, others will make them who may be ignorant of the service. If I say no they may get through anyway. If I change my mind and participate, it gives legitimacy to the activity. I've not resolved this at all.

Another manager said

I'm torn between hiding the cost of the cuts and keeping an adequate service going.

Despite these internal differences, the group's corporate stance, and image, was one of resistance as a means of exerting control to protect their areas of work.

In response to the first budgetary review, F.W. managers recommended reductions below the required level in their own division, and reductions in R. and D.C.. On the second occasion they recommended a percentage reduction in all their division's services. They refused to prioritise, unlike their senior management team leader, who presented an alternative paper, which identified priorities. They refused to accept information on reduction recommendations because it was confidential and they could not share it with their staff.

They voiced their opposition to reductions to senior management, R. and D.C. management, staff and politicians. They were critical of the process whereby the expenditure reviews were effected, and of the stance of co-operation. They requested and obtained a meeting with the councillor in charge of Social Services to air their grievances, and referred clients to this individual when an area office was closed by industrial action. They lobbied politicians. There were allegations from senior management and politicians that F.W.M.T. leaked information to the press on reduction recommendations. They also supplied councillors who sat on the Social Services Committee with a report on the effects of proposed reductions.

Services were withdrawn twice ('blacking') in line with the union's (N.A.L.G.O.) policy of refusing to do the work of posts which were left vacant to save money (the managed vacancy element). On one occasion an area office was temporarily closed because a supervisory post was vacant. On another occasion and in a different office, a vacant filing clerk's post resulted in files not being removed from the cabinets.

After the budget was known, F.W. managers continued to voice opposition and rejected a managing role in relation to the effects of reductions. Though it was clearly an issue, they discussed expenditure reductions management on only one occasion, in response to the paper referred to above. They also refused an offer from their team leader of responsibility for financial control.

Thus whilst within the ·team there was some uncertainty as to whether to co-operate and participate, or resist and withdraw, the majority of strategies members adopted were classified as examples of resistance and withdrawal. As such they reflect the independent non-directed nature of this group's sub-culture.

A professional rationality was apparent as most members defined themselves in terms of the social work profession, whose task was the identification of, and provision for, unmet needs. Reductions were perceived as being in direct conflict with this. Thus one member described reductions as a

dismantling of the service,

and another as

a suppression of need.

Managers, I was told, had a duty to oppose a further reduction in the circumstance of their client group, the disadvantaged. As they were at the sharp end of the community, they were aware of increased need due to the current unemployment situation. Reductions would limit their ability to provide help and they would become apologists for the system's lack of provision.

The majority of F.W. managers did not define their management task to include the management of expenditures reduction. In discussing their team leader's document on managing the effects of reductions, the responsibility for establishing priorities was raised.

A number of comments suggested that establishing priorities was essential for the management of reductions. Thus members made the following points:

It begs the question of priorities (for example) how to balance an assistant social worker with a home-help; these need to be looked at;

We need some mechanism to sort cases out;

It seems fairly complacent about how we make decisions: there's no prioritisation of work.

There was however disagreement about whether prioritisation was appropriate or not, and whether it was possible at a time of reductions. One F.W. manager made the point that

social services are too soft in dealing with other department's problems. We can't always say yes: we need to say no.

As an example, he instanced marital problems as an area his team no longer dealt with; other members said that they prioritised in a `crude way'. I was told privately for example that work with children had a higher priority than work with the elderly or handicapped. There was no direct link to expenditure reductions here though; informal prioritising had taken place before their advent. One member, whilst agreeing that he prioritised already, said that this should and could not be done to any greater extent. Whilst some members felt that `a review of the service would be useful' it would be impossible `in the climate of the cuts'. An alternative, and more popular view is represented by the statement that

> Prioritisation is against everything I stand for. We're not in the business of rationing or refusing services.

And the team did not prioritise services.

The team rejected this aspect of managing reductions and assigned it to the D.M.T. as the following quotations from F.W. managers indicate.

> It's appalling there is no guidance from the top;

> that bloody director and his useless management team provided no corporate plan or priorities;

> the D.M.T. should prioritise, should set out objectives; I don't think they've done any work, they're not motivated. They say its important but there's no evidence in terms of work on departmental priorities between community and residential care.

F.W. managers did not consider they had had any guidance from or had priorities established `from the top'. They were highly critical of this, and attempted to rectify it by requests to the D.M.T. for guidance as indicated earlier in this chapter.

Thus whilst the relevance of strategic rationality was recognised as important by some members if reductions were to be `managed', the majority F.W.M.T. view rejected strategic planning as a task for middle management. The D.M.T.'s use of administrative rationality was recognised and rejected. One member referred to

> the Director's strategy: push the `agro' down to the third tier (middle management) level.

It was the F.W.M.T.'s view that the D.M.T. should set priorities, and thus decide what was not to be provided.

Yet F.W. managers reported that they continued to manage the provision of service and `deal with the effect of reductions daily'. They did not reject their management task in total. They rejected those aspects which were formally introduced as changes to their task as a result of reductions. Thus they were not prepared formally, that is, as a management team, to consider and agree a corporate strategy on priorities, or reductions management generally. Similarly they rejected the formal offer of financial control of areas for which they had the spending responsibility.

Ideological rationality was based on opposition to the Conservative Government's strategy of reducing public expenditure. This approach was summarised by one F.W.M.T. member who said

> we fundamentally disagree with government policy on public services. We see no justification to reduce them or any moral defence. The policy is wrong-headed and inhuman.

Thus resistance at the local level was based on ideological opposition to the Government. Similarly, another member saw resistance as providing support for those local politicians who were themselves resisting reductions.

`Following the union line' and `protecting jobs' were both offered as reasons for resistance by F.W. managers. The former involved the withdrawals of service referred to earlier. It was also said, by some F.W. managers, to involve the avoidance of any team discussions of the issue of managing reductions. And apart from one occasion, the subject was not discussed.

Privately, though, a number of members expressed a need to discuss the management of reductions. The following points were made in support of this:

> the situation is desperate: we're sitting on a volcano;

> some prescriptions for action are needed;

> It's all happening in an implicit way with no discussion.

It was also one of the two most popular items to emerge from an agenda setting exercise which the team did. Some members, however, stated that union instructions precluded any such discussions. Managers' relations with staff would be adversely affected, they felt, if the latter perceived the team as not following the union directive.

In terms of job protection, one member said that managed vacancies were `the thin edge of the wedge'. If the division continued to work as usual, with a higher percentage of vacancies, temporary vacancies would become permanent ones. There was therefore a need to be seen not to manage. Overall then, the majority of members supported the union line, both in terms of their own position as union members, and as managers.

Political rationality, defined as recommending reductions which cannot be accepted because they are too politically sensitive, was referred to above when describing R. and D.C.M.T.'s budgetary strategy. F.W.M.T. were also keen for reductions to be seen as unacceptable, by detailing their effects. They thus provided councillors with information on the predicted effects of reductions on the range of the division's services, after the Department, (through the D.M.T.), had made its recommendations but before councillors had reached a decision. Unlike R. and D.C.M.T., they did not recommend specific politically sensitive reductions.

Additionally resistance was used by some members as a means of spotlighting the predicted effects, invariably negative, of reductions. To behave as instructed, to recommend reductions and to manage `with the least effect on the service' was described by F.W. managers in the following terms: `to mask', `to minimise', `to hide' the effect and the reality of reductions.

> A little here and a little there, there is nothing large to grab hold of

was how one manager described the strategy of reductions, which accords with the senior management description provided earlier in this chapter.In fact, reductions and their effects should not be hidden, but should be `maximised', `highlighted', and `dramatised'. Not managing as instructed was a way of doing this. As one F.W. manager put it

> F.W.'s idea was not to manage cuts, or hide them away by trimming here and there.

Unlike their R. and D.C. colleagues, F.W. managers chose means other than budgetary or organisational to do this.

Whilst the majority of managers described their budgetary strategies In terms of political rationality - exerting control by presenting the unacceptable - a minority of managers suggested that the team had used bureaucratic rationality initially, in recommending some reductions in their own, and other, divisions.

There was little time - we followed orders

was how one manager described their response. In this instance, initial shock (Fink et al: 1971) resulted in the group following orders. This response was found to be unacceptable when they had time to consider the implications of the instruction to recommend reductions.

F.W.M.T. adopted different strategies before and after their budget allocations had been decided. Whilst a number of F.W. activities during the pre-budget period, such as closing an area office, fall into the fight category of defensive action (Bion: 1961) some managers described the post-budget strategy of not discussing reductions management in terms of denial, or defensive retreat.

For example, one manager said

people close their eyes, they want to forget and are complacent about the cuts to come and the detailed implication of those already made. The whole area is difficult to grapple with, and there's a tendency to `leave well alone'.

Another said

If we keep quiet the whole thing might go away.

Yet another described his colleagues as operating a

massive denial.

Given the complexity of the matter, the differences of opinion and the variety of rationalities at work, it is perhaps not surprising that they did not grapple with the problem. Another member said simply, that they were

> sick of the subject (of reductions).

Another aspect of denial was evidenced by members who said they did not know what to do. One said

> perhaps in some situations there's nothing you can do.

Another said

> previously we were in a growth paradigm: I know the constituents and how to operate it. I felt comfortable with it. I had prescriptions for action. Now fundamental changes have occurred. We are in a different situation but I still have the same prescriptions for action. I don't know what to do.

Because reductions dramatically altered the management situation, traditional prescriptions for action were irrelevant. Managers were unsure how to behave in the absence of new prescriptions to deal with the change.

A number of authors support the view that decline management is significantly different from growth management. Levine (1978) states that

> organisations cannot be cut back merely by reversing the sequence of activities and resource allocation by which their parts were originally assembled. Decline forces us to set some of our logic for structuring organisations on its head and upside down (p. 317).

Much the same point is made by Glassberg (1978) and Mitnick (1978). Scott (1974), Green (1974), and Boulding (1975) regard decline as necessitating new skills and new arrangements in areas of financial and general management.

The D.M.T. argued that F.W. managers should do as R. and D.C. managers did: manage and co-operate. But F.W. managers were in a different, and more difficult position. Further discussion of these differences will be presented in subsequent chapters and in particular Chapter 8.

Two final points emerge from this explication of strategies and the rationalities underpinning them. The first concerns members' construction of an organisational history whereby various strategies of each middle management team were categorised as either co-operating or resisting. The second concerns the nature of resistance and withdrawal as revealed by this data, compared to the coverage of the subject in the literature on decline.

There were aspects of F.W.M.T.'s response that do not immediately seem to qualify as resistance activities, such as recommending some reductions, managing on a daily basis, and providing information on the effects of reductions. Similarly R. and D.C.M.T. resisted reductions by various budgetary strategies. Two factors seem to have influenced the discounting of this disconfirming information: one relates to the focus of the strategies adopted; the other to the use of pre-existing perceptions of group cultures, or how a group was 'expected' to behave.

R. and D.C.M.T. used the budgetary system and resisted within its confines unlike their F.W. colleagues. Thus whilst both groups acted in terms of political rationality, the focus of the resulting strategies determined the construction of responses as co-operating and resisting. The perceived culture of each group prior to reductions supported this construction. R. and D.C.M.T. was seen as bureaucratic, and F.W.M.T. as independent and questioning. Constructions of reduction strategies conformed to these preconceptions.

Resistance as a response is infrequently examined in the literature on decline. When acknowledged it is usually presented as predictable, short-lived and based on self-interest. Thus Levine (1978) states

> no organisation faces cuts with enthusiasm and will find
> ways to resist them (p. 320).

Biller (1976) and Behn (1976) make the same point. For Hall and Mansfield (1971) resistance is

> the early stage of coping with stress (p. 534).

Levine (1978) predicts disaster resulting from long-term resistance. Biller (1980) and Greenhalgh and McKersie (1980) make the same point as Caiden (1980):

where their own sphere of action is concerned they (politicians and officials) will fiercely resist cuts and seek to protect their own positions (p. 154).

This presentation of resistance is unsatisfactory on a number of grounds. Different management groups responded differently: there was no monolithic response. Nor was resistance an automatic response; there was no question of the R. and D.C.M.T. 'fiercely' resisting for example. Though the authors do not specify a time limit, it is assumed they mean a shorter period than the twelve months that the F.W.M.T. resisted. Resistance for F.W.M.T. achieved some positive results: two posts were filled rather than being left vacant; and two-thirds of the original recommended reduction was added back to their budget. Finally justifications other than self interest were evident.

This last point is recognised by a minority of authors. Thus Glennester (1980) refers to 'values and professional standards' (p.377) as causing defensive response. Wilburn and Worman (1980) remark:

> managers who have spent careers developing policies and programmes will, of course, fiercely resist major changes to their programmes (p. 612).

In fact it is clear from the data presented above that there are a number of reasons why managers did or did not resist reductions.

Hirschman (1970) identifies resistance as a useful and legitimate strategy, which he terms 'voice': it is

> any attempt at all to change, rather than escape from an objectionable state of affairs (p. 30).

Escaping, that is, leaving the organisation, he terms 'exit'. 'Voice' is likely to occur when members are attached to the organisations goals and it can lead to change and performance maintenance. It is not a strategy though that can be pursued indefinitely. Recognising that resistance is a legitimate strategy forms a more useful basis for its analysis, rather than in dismissing it as being expected, as short-lived, as based on self-interest alone, and as having negative outcomes if pursued for any period. Similarly Hirschman (1970) is one of the few authors writing on decline who recognise some form of management withdrawal as a response to decline. He uses the term boycott to describe a withdrawal of labour. In the organisation under consideration members of F.W.M.T. rejected or withdrew from tasks associated with expenditure reductions, but did not totally withdrawing from the organisation. The data thus expands the work of Hirschman by identifying a further category of response: withdrawal from a task area.

In addition to the data already presented, withdrawal behaviour was noted on the part of F.W. managers at a general level. Thus the F.W. team leader said

> Traditionally F.W. wants to be involved in everything; R. and D.C. don't. Now R. and D.C. is more involved than F.W..

Similarly, the R. and D.C. team leader said

> F.W. is less keen to participate in a cost conscious atmosphere.

Two authors writing on organisations in crisis refer to withdrawal and to control being handed over to superiors, either to avoid stress (Hermann: 1963) or to cope with uncertainty (Billings et al: 1980). Withdrawal was perceived by F.W. managers as a response to stress - a `difficult' area - and uncertainty - `I don't know what to do'. Additionally, though, it was seen by some F.W. managers as a strategy both to reduce the possibility of reductions and to expose their effects. Prescriptions for managing decline clearly then need to take into account the possibility that managers may withdraw from reduction related tasks in the ways and for the reasons described above.

Summary

This chapter outlines the different strategies adopted by the organisation's three management teams in response to expenditure reductions and presents the variety of rationalities underpinning them. The data does not support the view that expenditure reductions automatically lead to strategic rationality, as predicted by organisational monetarism. The significant influence of a group's culture on the management of decline was noted, and examples of defensive reactions such as avoidance, overt resistance and withdrawal, were provided. The literature on resistance to decline was examined, and found to be incomplete in that resistance was invariably described only as the initial, short-term response based on self interest. Finally, Hirschman's (1970) concept of withdrawal was expanded to include partial withdrawal as exemplified by F.W. managers' refusal to carry out reduction related tasks.

6 Interpretations of the managerial role in expenditure reductions

Introduction

This chapter considers managers' interpretations of their roles in respect of expenditure reductions and organisational changes which resulted from the onset of financial stringency.

In discussing responses to reductions, managers generalised these into two broad categories: co-operation and resistance. Managers' descriptions used a number of concepts which provided a means of analysing different interpretations of the managerial role. The ways in which these concepts - realism, responsibility, values, maturity, caring, emotionalism and participation - were defined and applied indicated that the managerial role may be interpreted in significantly different ways. These interpretations accorded with the sub-culture of each group. The use of these concepts to describe and evaluate managerial action is considered below, together with the degree to which managers were certain their actions were appropriate.

Managers performed their tasks within a number of fora in the organisation: their own area of responsibility, their management team, and their division. Less frequently they were involved in cross divisional meetings of middle managers and departmental meetings of both middle and senior managers. Interaction in each of these was seen to change adversely with stringency. These changes are examined below.

Initially all managers' responded negatively on an emotional level. Intra and inter group conflict increased. In addition F.W.managers' perceived their authority with staff undermined, the control they were subject to increased, and their division devalued. The advent of reductions produced a number of organisational changes which were not predicted by the concept of organisational monetarism.

Differing Realities or Myths

Realistic was a term used by some co-operators to define their activities, which one R. and D.C. manager said

> showed the ability of R. and D.C. to grasp the reality of the
> situation rather than the philosophical implications.

Reality here was defined as the practical implications' of the situation. Another member described reality as follows:

> they (the cuts) were not going to go away.

They were `inevitable' said a third. Those who resisted involvement, who `took no part' were `burying their heads in the sand' and were `ostrich-like'. Thus realism involved accepting, rather than ignoring, the practical implications of expenditure reductions, and putting the philosophical implications to one side.

Whilst recognising the `reality' of reductions, and the element of withdrawal in their own behaviour, F.W. managers did not describe themselves as unrealistic. They regarded their own actions as both a means of changing and exposing reality. One F.W. manager said, for example, that

> resources are not given, like the weather; they can be
> changed by action.

As we saw in the previous chapter, not managing was regarded as a way of highlighting the reality of reductions, and their effects, rather than hiding these, as a co-operative stance was seen to do. In addition, F.W. managers laid claim to a stronger reality base for their actions derived from their position at the interface with the client community.

In fact each group attempted to exert influence towards change, an influence based on their own definitions of the reality of expenditure reductions. The primary focus of reality for R. and D.C.M.T. was the instruction to recommend reductions which would have least effect on the service. Their reality was that defined by the senior management and councillors, which focused on the financial management task and relied heavily on the parameters of the budgetary process. Reality for F.W.M.T. involved definitions additional to those supplied by senior management and as a result reality was more complex and problematic.

For example, the F.W. division was heavily unionised at both staff and management level. N.A.L.G.O.'s policy as indicated in Chapter V, was one of non-co-operation with the management of reductions. Thus one aspect of F.W. managers' reality was the negative attitude of staff to reductions management. As one F.W. manager said,

> the notion of management is not based on the reality of the union attitude. You can prioritise all you like, but if there's no co-operation, no system is operable.

That this was a factor influencing F.W.'s reality was recognised by R. and D.C. managers. It was not a factor with R. and D.C. managers, as their staff were not unionised; each group then perceived reality differently.

Reality was more complex for F.W. managers because a number of constituents, in addition to their senior management team, were involved in defining the situation, and defining what was appropriate action. These additional constituents included staff, the union, and managers themselves both as individuals and as a group. Reality was problematic because there was no unity between constituents, particularly between senior management, and the others.

> Who do I listen to, my staff or senior management?

was how one F.W. manager put it, reflecting on his boundary role. Clearly the fundamental issue under consideration was who defined reality and the extent to which superiors' reality was the basis for managerial action. In particular the degree to which superiors' definition were accepted or not, largely determined whether particular situations were perceived as capable of being changed.

Differing realities also appeared significant in the attempt by senior management to undermine the resistor's reality, by pointing to the illusory nature of their objections. If they had operated in the past under similar circumstances, why should the present situation be so objectionable. Thus R. and D.C.M.T.'s leader pointed out that in the past

F.W. has underspent on salaries, so why all the fuss?

The F.W.M.T.'s leader made a similar point to his own team: the division had in the past worked with a similar vacancy element to that which they were experiencing with reductions. It was implied that their current situation was not so different, and therefore not so difficult, as managers believed it was.

This example provides an interesting variation on what Gouldner (1954) terms the Rebecca Myth, where current reality is defined by reference to a past golden age. Here the present is defined as being no worse than the past.

Responsibility

The terms `responsible' and `responsibility' were used by members of both groups to describe their activities as either responsibility for a task or responsibility for a significant reference group. How managers' defined their expenditure reductions task has been considered in Chapter 5. Briefly R. and D.C. managers accepted the task definition supplied by senior management:

Managers do what they're told from above.

Their F.W. colleagues did not:

> It's not our job to recommend cuts; higher management should decide that.

Management groups had different task definitions. Whilst R. and D.C. managers were certain that their definition was appropriate, their F.W. colleagues were far less certain.

A minority of F.W. managers, and in particular their team leader, felt their colleagues were responsible for taking action other than resistance and withdrawal. Their team leader, referring to the closure of an area office said

> It's dramatic but certain things have to be done; other responsibilities have to be taken into account.

The document he presented on managing reduction began and finished with reference to `responsible': his assumption was

> that all members of F.W.M.T. will exercise their responsibilities in relation to the management of their respective areas

and his support could be expected

> as long as decisions have been responsibly made.

`Responsibilities' indicated managing reductions whilst continuing to provide a service. Indeed, some members referred to their `management responsibilities' when describing reduction related tasks, which suggests that rejection of these tasks was not complete; there was some uncertainty. Another team member said that though his F.W. colleagues

> stopped that type of activity (recommending reductions)
> they were responsible to do something;

rather than withdrawing, they were `duty bound' to take some managerial action.

Levine (1978) states that

> no responsible manager wants to be faced with the prospect of being unable to control where cuts will take place (p. 320).

He does not define responsibility further but in the organisation under study a manager's responsibility was not invariably seen to include reductions related tasks; some F.W. managers defined their responsibility to include resisting expenditure reductions as a means of protecting the social work service.

'Responsibility' also concerned the significant reference group to whom middle managers were responsible. Members of R. and D.C.M.T., for example, made the following points:

> My responsibility is to the department who pay my salary. In a company, you do a job, or get the sack. Why is it different here?;

> An employee has an obligation to do the job. If they disagree, they should change their job. We carried out instructions;

> F.W. managers should implement cuts or resign.

The co-operators saw themselves as having a prime responsibility to their superiors by 'carrying out instructions'. The only alternative was resignation or what Hirschman (1970) terms 'exit'.

Reference amongst this group to other responsibilities, such as to staff, were infrequently made. Thus the Director said F.W. managers should

> take a third tier management view, not the view of other ranks.

A middle management view should be paramount. Its opposition to a staff view of reductions was recognised. An R. and D.C. manager said to F.W. managers

> You cross the fence when you become manager and cease to be a social worker. You're trying to run with the hare and the hounds.

A manager has no business taking into account a professional social work view, which was seen to be in opposition to the management perspective, that is, following orders. This latter quotation represents an extreme position, but it is nevertheless useful as indicating the way this group interpreted their role. Whilst professional values were a factor, this was overridden by a paramount responsibility towards senior management. The majority of F.W. managers perceived themselves as having responsibilities to a wider group than did their R. and D.C. colleagues. A F.W. manager said

> F.W. take a wider view and don't necessarily follow instructions.

Another manager said

> a problem with cuts was the difficulty of reconciling management responsibilities and personal values; the union position and political views.

A third said

> I feel my management responsibilities and my union responsibilities are difficult to reconcile.

There was then more than one significant reference group to which F.W. managers saw themselves responsible. In general though, they did not view their responsibility to senior management as outweighing other responsibilities.

Value Bases of Rationalities

In the previous chapter, the variety of rationalities in use were discussed. These are now explored further. An explanation offered for F.W. manager activities was the unacceptable influence of what were variously described by the co-operators as personal values, social values, political values and philosophical values. In effect these were values that were not in accord with those of senior management. R. and D.C. managers generally presented themselves as being free of any such unsanctioned influences. For example, one R. and D.C. manager said

> Perhaps I'm old-fashioned. I divide my job and my political values. I'm just doing a job. I leave my personal values at the door of the workplace...Privately I may agree (with opposition to the cuts) but as an officer, I do as I'm instructed.

Thus the employer has the prerogative of determining values in use at the workplace.

This claim to be uninfluenced by personal values at work is, however, in itself a value. As an approach to defining the manager's role, it side-steps the issue of conflicting values. That the same approach did not apply to F.W. managers was recognised; a member of R. and D.C.M.T. remarked

> some people in F.W. had a hell of a job reconciling their political and social values and their job.

Value conflict was an issue for F.W. managers, the majority of whom usually operated in tune with values other than those of their senior management. One F.W. manager said, for example,

> Attitudes to cuts are seen as representing a world view, an approach to life, but that's the way I approach things generally: I relate them to my values and political beliefs:

That is to say, personal values were brought into the workplace and rationalised.

That the R. and D.C.M.T. stance was seen as value-free, but not approved of, was supported by the F.W. manager who described the former as

> Following orders, like Eichmann.

An interesting example of the assumed match between workplace and personal values was provided by an R. and D.C. manager. He reported the surprised reaction of a F.W. manager when they met at a Labour Party meeting. The latter did not expect to see the former there because of his managerial response to reductions:

126

He (the F.W. manager) assumed because of my action that I'd
vote Tory and march with the National Front.

In fact, some members of R. and D.C.M.T. did use values other than those of
senior management in evaluating reductions, and their own involvement in
them. A minority said that if things got too bad, that is unacceptable in terms
of their own values, they would do something. For example, one said

> If they closed all homes, then I'd do something. I didn't think
> the proposals were particularly drastic, not enough to
> warrant F.W.'s response.

This member had assessed the situation and found it acceptable in terms of
his own values, compromising perhaps along the way.

R. and D.C. managers referred to the use of political values by their
F.W. colleagues; political here being used to refer to action based on political
ideology. Political action was defined as action which attempted to influence
politicians and which was outside the normal channels of communication.
An example of a normal channel was the budgetary process. The co-
operators regarded the use of other channels as unacceptable in a manager;
the resistors as part of their management reality. Thus an R.and D.C.
manager said

> F.W. has a highly political view of their job, unlike R. and
> D.C. who keep well out of it.

It was

> the council's job to tell the Government where to go on cuts,
> not the staff's.

Another said

> F.W. managers used their political muscle to fight the
> council, they lobbied councillors.

127

Closing an area office was defined as a `political demonstration'. As we have seen, the integration of ideological values into workplace action was regarded as acceptable by F.W. managers.

In fact one member of R. and D.C.M.T. did refer to ideological values in reductions. He said

> The Conservatives have the right idea .... What's the alternative to cuts? I'd like to see Mrs Thatcher ask her opponents that.

This, though, was a minority view and generally R. and D.C.M.T.'s attitude was to `keep well out of it'.

The difference between resistors and co-operators was then about who defines values in use in the workplace. For the co-operators it was principally their superiors. In some instances there was an element of value convergence. For the resistors other values were also significant in determining action. Divergence between these and those of senior management led to dissonance which was resolved by taking action in terms of their own rather than their superiors' values.

The question of managers' values about whether it is ethical to manage decline or not, is infrequently addressed in the literature. Levine (1979) notes the effect on clients and employees of reduced finances, but he does not elaborate. The general assumption appears to be that managers will manage decline, whatever their beliefs. The rightness or wrongness of the issue, or how one moves from one to the other, has not commanded attention. Personal values, whether political, professional or social are seldom referred to. Those values which are considered concern the continued operation of the organisation in decline, by the imposition, or inculcation of new values, such as those of financial management (Cyert: 1975, 1978) or non-material rewards (Scott: 1976). On the whole the literature seems more concerned with identifying values which will facilitate decline management, rather than identifying and dealing with existing, pre-decline values, which may or may not facilitate the management of reductions.

A number of authors writing in the industrial relations field refer to value clashes. Flanders (1964) suggests that value clashes are the least susceptible to settlement by compromise. Eldridge (1968) points to the value base of competing rationalities in use by different groups in conditions of redundancy. He suggests that a plurality of values is a normal feature of industrial life, as does Fox (1969). In the organisations studied, plurality of values was not inevitably accepted as normal, yet pre-decline values which, at a collective level were evidence of a group's sub-culture, were seen to inhibit or facilitate the management of reductions.

Caring, Maturity and Strikes

Resistance was seen by R. and D.C. managers as indicating a non-caring attitude towards clients on the part of F.W. For example, one R. and D.C. manager said

> cuts strikes indicate the way social workers feel for clients. If they really cared for clients, they'd sign out cases themselves.

that is, they would by-pass normal administrative procedures. The R. and D.C. team leader said:

> Their (F.W. managers) action implies the service is more for them (F.W.) than clients. They strike, yet prophesy death and destruction if they're cut. Closing an area office only pressurises clients. What about the client in the F.W. strategy of freezing the work of vacant posts?.

Similarly resistance was seen as childish. Thus one R. and D.C. manager likened F.W.'s attitude to `a spoilt child - that's what I must have'. Another R. and D.C. manager said

> we realised there would be cuts whatever, and were more mature.

Their team leader said

> R. and D.C.M.T. handled cuts in a calm and adult way... they did not behave like retarded adolescents.

Thus for R. and D.C. managers, managing indicated a caring and mature attitude; resisting indicated the reverse.

F.W. managers did not interpret behaviour in quite the same way. For them, managing was an example of `complacency' and an uncaring attitude to staff and clients. Their own `strikes' were presented as being part of a strategy which would ultimately help clients, by challenging the presented need for reductions.

Members of both groups felt that `caring' was an acceptable aspect of the management role; differences were based on what action reflected this attribution. The mature-immature dimension was not used by F.W. managers either to describe their own or others' behaviour.

Emotional or Rational Responses

Both resistors and co-operators recognised emotions as having an unproductive influence on the management of expenditure reductions. Resistance and withdrawal were described as emotional responses which inhibited the F.W.M.T.'s effectiveness.

For example, one F.W. manager described his team's discussions of expenditure reductions as

> clouded with emotionalism and hot air.

Another said

> Reductions ...was an emotional issue which blocked off other work. We talked about emotion values, politics, but not the practical implications of the cuts.

Another manager, who wished the team would consider reductions management, suggested members `sit on their feelings', that is, control their emotions and thereby allow rational discussions to take place. Emotions inhibited a consideration of practical implications; the two were perceived to be in opposition.

No one argued for emotions as a prime determinant of action, and no one described R. and D.C. managers as emotional. Whilst the majority of managers reported that reductions produced an initial negative response, as we shall see later in the chapter, the extent to which these emotions were seen to influence management behaviour was the subject of criticism. There was general agreement that managers should not allow emotions to interfere with the task performance.

Participation or Control

Managers differed on whether they should control information or consult and involve subordinates.

F.W. managers generally interpreted their role to include information-sharing with staff. This was termed `open government'. Members objected to a diminution of their ability to be open by the classification of information as confidential. One member said

> with the cuts, the doors of openness seem to be closing.

As we saw in Chapter 5, the team refused confidential information because it could not be shared with subordinates. Another member said

> cuts is a time of secrets, lots of secrets. You feel you don't really know what's going on.

That is, there was a lack of information on reductions which resulted from it being withheld or classified as confidential. F.W. managers criticised their R. and D.C. colleagues because the latter did not

> inform their staff (of reduction proposals) because it would create insecurity. It's patronising and takes away the right to argue and advocate for oneself.

Another F.W. manager said

R. and D.C. measures were terrible. They talked of staff redeployment with no consultation. Their team leader argued that it was no good stirring up trouble with tentative proposals.

This justification was supported by one R. and D.C. manager:

I was told by John (the team leader) not to consult staff as it would worry them.

Another said:

I didn't consult staff as there was no time.

One member of R. and D.C.M.T. did share information with her immediate subordinates, in confidence, but the information itself was not subject to debate. In general, as we saw in Chapter 4, R. and D.C. managers saw consultation as being in opposition to action. They did not construct their role in such a way that it was seen as a `right' for staff. For F.W. managers, consultation was an integral part of the management task. As one F.W. manager said:

R. and D.C. managers tend to see decisions as management ones rather than as the result of consultation as we do in F.W..

In this instance, consultation was seen by one group as enabling staff to argue their case; it was seen by the other as resulting in unnecessary insecurity or worry. One group considered consultation to be a staff right: the other did not. This data supports the point made earlier that F.W. managers were more concerned than their R. and D.C. colleagues to take account of their staff's views.

At the senior management level, the control of information was infrequently seen to have a negative effect. One such effect was noted by the F.W. team leader. He said the D.M.T.'s priority of protecting R. and D.C. should have been made public at the time as F.W. felt `done in' and `ripped off' and in his view information on this priority would have reduced their reaction. Later in this chapter, F.W. managers `explanations' of their relatively adverse treatment is considered.

Within the literature there are observations of, or prescription for, both less and more participation or organisational democracy in times of reductions. Levine (1979) refers to the participation paradox as one of the problems peculiar to organisations in decline: participative decision-making may result in a protective behaviour on the part of those most affected. Cazalis (1979) doubts whether democratic procedures will be helpful in managing organisational austerity, for such procedures are in opposition to the goals of output, performance, and productivity. Whetton (1980: b) identifies the tendency of decision makers to reduce the amount of consultation in times of crisis and Bogue (1972) points out that the more consultation there is, the more open conflict there is.

Cyert (1975) on the other hand recommends participation and the sharing of information because it is through this process that

> the goal (of increased productivity) is incorporated into their
> own (staff's) goal structure (p. 12)

and greater organisational unity will result. Berger (1982) found, on the basis of studying fifty-three school districts which were experiencing decline, that

> generally participation will lead to greater commitment and
> less resistance (p. 338).

Gill and Pratt (1986) suggest that participative, decentralised allocation discussions in conditions of declining resources are advantageous as they stimulate creativity and the production of information. The actual allocation decision may however have to be made by an authority figure. Hirschhorn (1983: a) suggests that it is

> better to disclose information (p. 28),

to

> reveal bad news to the staff (p. 24)

133

in order to reduce uncertainty, and he makes much the same point in a discussion of the negative effects of rumour in decline (Hirschhorn: 1983: c).

The advisability and practicality of participative decision-making in respect of expenditure reductions is arguable (for example: Levine: 1978). The significant point which emerges from this case however, is that staff participation, or lack of it, was regarded as important by only one management group. This seemed to depend on whether or not participation and consultation were an aspect of a particular management group's sub-culture and thus whether participation was a taken for granted aspect of managerial activity. The conditions imposed by senior management (secrecy and non-consultation) were inimical to the F.W. managers' normal method of managing. Conversely, these conditions matched those already in existence in R. and D.C.M.T. because management by directive was a normal aspect of their sub-culture. Thus for F.W.M.T. managing expenditure reduction involved not only task issues, such as deciding what to reduce, but also process issues of how this task was carried out; whether, in effect, they should accept or reject a new, non- participative, style of management.

Managers' Evaluations of `Right' and `Wrong'

It will have become clear that different responses to reductions were explicitly evaluated as right and wrong. Firstly, a F.W. manager said responses became `a way of judging people in the organisation', that is, different responses provided data on which an evaluation of members could legitimately be made. Secondly, a number of managers pointed out that justifications for alternative responses involved a `holier than thou' attitude, that is, one particular response was not only different but better than another. One R. and D.C. manager said that both his own team, and F.W. managers adopted this attitude. Thus different responses were presented and perceived in terms of right and wrong, rather than as equally valid, but different, management responses.

Managerial Role Interpretations

Different interpretations of the middle management role revolved around who defined reality, management values and task, and the limits of participation. For R. and D.C. managers, their superiors were seen to have the prerogative in this process. For F.W. managers, other groups were seen as legitimately influential in addition to senior management. As they provided conflicting definitions, both conflict and confusion resulted.

The co-operative response was described by its adherents as indicating maturity, and both groups claimed their actions indicated a caring attitude towards clients; neither espoused emotions as a legitimate influencing factor. Both groups evaluated their own responses as right, and the alternative as wrong, though amongst F.W. managers there was far less certainty.

In terms of the action which resulted from these interpretations, R. and D.C. managers `followed orders', that is, managed reductions within the definition provided by senior management. F.W. managers rejected this definition and challenged the assumption that their superiors had the prerogative to define and change the management role.

Role interpretation can be seen to reflect taken for granted rules of managing. At the collective level, the espousal of similar rules reflects the sub-culture of a particular management group. Different role interpretations broadly match differences between managerial sub-cultures, in, for example, a preference for participative, or directive relations with staff. It was apparent that role problems resulted from the dissonance between the role as defined in terms of a group's sub-culture, and the role as defined by senior management in respect of managing expenditure reductions. Thus members of R. and D.C.M.T. saw their role as unproblematic because no significant change from their normal, pre-reductions way of managing was required: there was fit between what senior management required, and how R. and D.C. managers usually interpreted and performed their role. F.W. managers, on the other hand, regarded the degree of dissonance between their usual management performance and the new one demanded by senior management as problematic, for it challenged their taken for granted managerial activity which, until the advent of reductions, was regarded as successful.

Leaving aside 'exit' (Hirschman: 1970), there appeared to be four alternatives open to F.W. managers to reduce this dissonance, three of which they specified:

1) accept a re-defined management role in terms of senior management's instructions;

2) ignore disconfirming information (senior management instructions) and therefore the need to adapt one's role;

3) attempt to change the situation and redefine the role.

Of these three, the first was used temporarily at the beginning of the reduction process and subsequently was not seriously considered by the majority of F.W. managers. A mixture of the second and third alternatives were adopted, though neither of these were cost or problem free. The fourth alternative, managerial pragmatism or contingency management - the notion that managers can carry out their role in different ways, depending on the particular circumstances to be managed - was not one that found much, if any, support amongst F.W. managers, or for that matter, managers generally in the organisation. Rather, the interpretation of the manager's role was by mutually exclusive, either/or categories: for example, managers either invariably supported participation by staff or they were invariably directive towards staff; they were not particularly flexible.

A further source of unease for F.W. managers were the changes in behaviour caused by the move away from their preferred ideal, which were noted in F.W.M.T. meetings where the group's culture was defined and redefined. Managers linked these changes causally to the advent of expenditure reductions and this is described below.

Organisational Changes

F.W. managers perceived changes to the fora within which they performed their tasks, as a result of expenditure reductions. They identified change in their management team, their individual areas, and the department as a whole. Problems identified were: an increase in intra and intergroup conflict and competition; an under-mining of managers' authority with staff; increased central control; and the negative interpretation placed on differential reductions. For R. and D.C.M.T. and D.M.T. the main outcomes of resource reductions were the short-term distractions of producing recommendations, and the longer term conflict with F.W.M.T. Additionally, as we saw in Chapter 5, the D.M.T. experienced internal disagreement about strategic planning.

These differences indicate that the nature or extent of change which a reduction in expenditure was designed to impose was not uniformly perceived by management groups. The greater the change involved, the greater difficulty the group had in managing this change.

Organisational Climate and Group Cohesiveness

On one matter there was general agreement amongst managers at senior and middle levels; namely that reductions occasioned negative rather than positive feelings. Even the manager who supported reductions ideologically confessed to having a `few sleepless nights'. It was said to be an `emotional and depressing time'. Another R. and D.C. manager said it was a time of

Tension, anxiety and low morale.

Another referred to:

uncertainty and insecurity.

Similarly a F.W. manager said:

cuts were terrible. I can't remember the details. I've blocked them off.

Another said:

> Oh God what a mess ... It was very stressful ...with a great air
> of despondency. The organisation paid the price in terms of
> morale.

Even the Director recognised that reductions were 'difficult and traumatic for staff', though he qualified this by saying

> some people see disaster before it comes.

No-one said it was a time of harmony, high morale or new opportunities.

The exception was an initial fighting spirit and cohesion which brought in-group members together in the face of an external enemy, a feature noted by both F.W. and R. and D.C. management team members. Thus some F.W. managers referred to a 'Battle of Britain Spirit' and 'a feeling of going to war' which was apparent when the group was initially involved in expenditure reductions. Similarly as we saw in Chapter 5, R. and D.C.M.T. organised themselves into cohesive groups in response to the threat from F.W.M.T. Increased group solidarity is noted by Coser (1956) as a positive function of social conflict. Similarly Staw et al (1981) predict an increase in intra group cohesiveness in the face of a threat ('impending loss or cost to the entity' (p. 503)). This though will be short-lived if the group fails to meet the challenge. Social Services managers noted this fighting spirit was dissipated over time. The F.W.M.T. became competitive, untrusting and divided, as members competed for resources and disagreed about their joint strategy to deal with reductions. R. and D.C.M.T. 'became sick of it, it was silly', and cohesiveness was reduced by lack of interest.

Cohesiveness was reduced in F.W.M.T. by dissension about how to deal with the threat, rather than an experience of failure. Strategy to deal with threat, which Staw et al (1981) treat as unproblematic, can itself be a divisive issue. Similarly, R. and D.C.M.T.'s cohesiveness resulted from their agreement on strategy to meet the threat. Though this strategy was successful, cohesion was short-lived due to members' lack of interest. This contradicts Staw et al's predictions that, with success, cohesion is likely to be longer lived, and at a higher level; a threat response strategy can be a significant factor in increasing or decreasing group cohesiveness. This apparently flows from the extent to which there is agreement on how to meet the outside challenge, rather than, as Staw et al suggest, the ultimate success or failure of the strategy.

Intragroup Competition

Members of the F.W.M.T. drew a distinction between approaches to resource allocation which focused on corporate or divisional needs and that which focused on individualistic or area needs. They perceived an opposition between these two approaches, and stated a preference for the former. Corporateness was a group value, an aspect of sub-culture. This value was challenged by the reductions task, and its behavioural utility was abandoned in practice. Some members were unsure how to construct their role in this respect:

> I'm torn between my area needs and the corporate management of resources;

> I'm torn between what's good for the F.W.M.T. and what's good for my own area;

> It's more difficult to be corporate with scarce resources.

The majority of team members saw a move towards individualism and away from the preferred corporate approach. This was linked to an increase in competition between members. As one manager said

> It's easy to have goodwill if there's plenty of resources: now relations are strained: its the law of the jungle.

This was supported by fellow team members, who made the following remarks: each member was

> rooting for their own area.

> The management team is breaking up with competition for resources;

139

fighting over scarce resources is adversely influencing the F.W.M.T....

One member who supported the ideal of a corporate approach said

At the moment, I'm frantically advertising posts as they come up. I feel it's every man for himself and I'm sure others do too. I've no intention of being a lamb to the slaughter by holding my vacancies open while others fill theirs.

This suggests that when resources are reduced, consumption goes up, at least until the money runs out, because individual consumers do not wish to lose resources to their colleagues. This `every man for himself' approach assumes that colleagues are responding in much the same way. Financial restraint is equated with sacrifice, and may ultimately lead to unfilled vacancies for managers who adopt that approach. Corporate management values were superceded in practice as members competed for resources on an individual basis and the sub-culture of the group was challenged and undermined by responses to reductions management.

Thus resource reductions led to increased competition. No one approached suggested that reductions presented new opportunities for a consideration of the most effective and/or efficient use of resources. Changes were noted, but towards individualism and competition. This suggests that corporate management may be very difficult to maintain in times of resource scarcity; and that changes in the group's sub-culture behaviour were precipitated by the introduction of reductions. A decrease in trust within the team was also noted, and this too was linked to competition as the following quotations indicate:

The F.W. group is more competitive; there's a lack of trust in the management team;

It's easy to be open whilst the service is developing. It's difficult with cuts.

The team became divided:

140

cuts brought out the cracks in group solidarity and highlighted division. F.W.M.T. has divided into small groups. It feels like a shambles now

was how one member put it. Another said:

F.W.M.T. is less cohesive; there's been a polarisation from defensiveness, it's less cohesive. In stress situations people tend to adopt extreme positions rather than being somewhere in the middle. It's everyone for themselves and their allies.

They had splintered because the issues of reductions management and resource competition highlighted pre-existing divisions.

The leader's relations with the F.W.M.T. were affected by these internal divisions for, as one member put it,

cuts opened up our differences with David (the F.W.M.T. leader) .... He was more accepting of the Director's and D.M.T.'s way to play it.

That is, he wanted his team to manage reductions; the majority of members wished to avoid this and the group was thus separated from its leader and vice versa.

Intragroup competition was not a feature of expenditure reductions noted by R. and D.C. managers. Internal unanimity was in fact increased temporarily in response to a threat from F.W.M.T. Thus the advent of expenditure reductions does not inevitably lead to intragroup competition and conflict. R. and D.C. managers were brought closer to their team leader because they shared the super-ordinate goal (the Sherifs: 1953) of managing expenditure reductions as instructed.

Intergroup Conflict

At the inter-divisional level, members of all three management teams notes an increase in conflict between F.W.M.T. and R. and D.C.M.T.. As one senior manager put it

> cuts have produced a nadir in inter-divisional relationships.

Similarly the relations between F.W.M.T. and the D.M.T. moved towards conflict. A F.W. manager said

> Before (reductions) we always worked in co-operation with senior management. Now I see it getting more conflictual.

The F.W. team leader suggested that this was because

> differences are thrown into relief by the cuts issue because the positions taken, the attitudes adopted, are more trenchant; day-to-day working shows up differences less starkly.

The contrasting of reductions as an issue with `day-to-day workings' indicates that the former can be classified as what Pettigrew (1979) terms a `social drama 'and also confirms Hermann's (1963) hypothesis that

> a crisis will tend to intensify any conflict existing prior to the crisis (p. 68).

In addition though, reductions as an issue created conflict by introducing a new element to the management role about which there was strong disagreement.

Within the literature there is some consensus that conflict increases with resource scarcity. A number of authors, such as Levine (1978 and 1979) and Scott (1974) base their explanation of this on Cyert and March's (1963) concept of slack resources which are used to buy organisational consensus. Increased conflict therefore results from decreased resources. Some authors focus on the use to which resources are put, or goals. Gill (1981), in the case of Higher Educational organisations, uses Cyert and March's (1963) notion of organisations having poorly defined goals. With scarcity, strategic goals become the subject of debate and conflict is generated.

In this instance though, reductions introduced a new and additional set of conflicting goals. At an intragroup level, competition for resources promoted disharmony in the F.W.M.T. In addition, differences on how to respond to reductions promoted conflict and it was the intergroup level which was the main topic of conversation amongst managers. Goal differences principally related to those who accepted involvement in reductions as a legitimate goal, and those who did not. Thus analyses which focus only on resources, and the purpose for which these are used, do not fully explain managers' responses.

Intergroup conflict is not though the inevitable outcome of stringency. There was no conflict between R. and D.C.M.T. and the D.M.T. because they shared a superordinate goal (the Sherifs: 1953): that of managing expenditure reductions. In this instance harmony rather than conflict resulted from the imposition of resource reductions.

Managerial Authority

The instruction to manage reductions was seen by some F.W. managers to undermine their ability to exert influence over staff. The attitude of their staff to reductions was, as we have seen, a significant factor for F.W. managers in determining their own responses. Managers also saw these attitudes as directly influencing their ability to manage staff. One manager said

> the strength of my credibility depends on my reaction to cuts.

Another termed this

> the limit of authority.

He went on to explain

> in the office I feel under surveillance to see if I'm conforming with the union line. Managers need to retain the co-operation

of their area teams. You can't work in isolation from the team. If there's any further action on management's part, we cannot count on the staff.

Credibility and authority were thus seen to depend on boycotting reductions; the latter manager referring to this as an `impossible restraint'. Managers could either become alienated from staff by managing, or alienated from senior management and their R. and D.C. colleague, by resisting reductions. Though they chose the latter they were still `under surveillance', that is, a lack of trust had developed within area teams which made the management task less easy to perform.

Strengthening of Managerial Control

A number of F.W. managers noted the increased control exerted by the D.M.T. and the Director in reductions whilst R. and D.C. managers did not refer to this as a significant issue. In addition to control of information F.W. managers made the following points:

> The D.M.T. is more involved in the day-to-day running of the organisation: we put more things up (for approval) and lose more than previously: third-tier management has less autonomy;

> the cuts gave him (the Director) a reason to `come into his own,' to stop any project: money.

> The Director is now more powerful than anyone else.

Fewer resources were thus seen to decrease middle management autonomy because more items needed the approval of senior management than previously and this increased the Director's power.

F.W.'s team leader attempted to increase his own, and his team's, management control by recommending they adopt a number of financial control measures, including a regular review of spending, both centrally by the team leader, and by the team. Details of these proposals are found in Chapter 5.

Within the literature, increase in control is considered by Hamblin (1958) who states that crisis provides organisational leaders with an opportunity to centralise control. Pfeffer and Leblebici (1973) point out that organisations respond to external pressure by calling for more and better management. Cazalis (1979) suggests increased control as a means of increasing productivity. Cyert (1978) recommends strong leadership to deal with decline and Levine et al (1981) discovered that management of decline is more effective with 'more centralised control' (p. 620). Thus stronger control is either observed, predicted or recommended as a means of managing decline, stress and crisis.

It may appear paradoxical that members who offered up control by withdrawal, as noted earlier, should object to control being taken away. Billings et al (1980) suggest that centralisation is facilitated by subordinates relinquishing control. In fact, and again as noted earlier, it was the task of managing reductions, and, in particular, prioritising services that was unwanted, not management control more generally. Thus despite withdrawing, some F.W. managers felt unhappy about what they saw as control in general being taken away; they wanted it both ways.

Differential Reductions

The F.W. division experienced greater reductions than the R. and D.C. division. This was interpreted by members of F.W.M.T. as representing a negative evaluation of their work, of them as individuals, and of past behaviour.

As an introduction to interpretations placed upon differential reductions, the following quotation from a F.W. manager is instructive:

> As cuts were across the board (that is, they were applied to all departments) they are not regarded by the Director as a personal attack on him, his department or his status.

This provides an insight into how reductions that were not applied across the board could be interpreted.

One F.W. member said reductions represented the

Council's turn-around in its attitude to Social Services.

That is, reductions represented a negative evaluation of the work area affected. Another said

the Director is not keen on the profession of social work

as an interpretation of why F.W. had been reduced more than R. and D.C.

The individuals involved in obtaining resources were evaluated by subordinates in terms of the amount they obtained or retained. As one F.W. manager put it

the resources I get determine my status in the area.

Fewer resources therefore meant reduced status, and another F.W. manager made a similar point in relation to their team leader:

The AD was on show. If he's good, we'll get less cuts than them (R. and D.C.), if not we get more.

Because they got more cuts, their leader was defined as less good. Conversely, the fact that R. and D.C. had `done well' was seen to reflect the competence of their leader.

Some members saw greater reductions in their division as a sanction against past bad behaviour. A F.W. manager said the extent of reductions were

seen to be a sanction for incompetence: you've done badly, so you get less, as a punishment for not toeing the line or for stepping out of line

with regard to reductions management. Because F.W.M.T. resisted involvement they were financially penalised. Conversely, fewer cuts were seen as a reward for correct behaviour.

Reductions were also seen by some managers as retribution on the Director's part for the behaviour of the previous leader of F.W.M.T. who undermined the Director's power position by consulting directly with councillors. The team's new leader was seen as less powerful. With the advent of reductions the Director was said by one F.W. manager to be

> glad to do F.W. down as their power is no longer in evidence.

Additionally, this previous team leader was said, by a number of F.W. managers, to be

> an incrementalist, who grabbed resources in any way he could.

Some felt he had, as one member put it:

> ripped the department off.

Fewer resources for F.W. was seen as a `settling of old scores'. One manager said

> F.W. assumed that they would be ripped off - it's rough justice because of the past.

This past was also used to explain the response by non-members to reductions in F.W.

> Perhaps people feel F.W.'s done O.K. in the last few years and they deserve everything they got.

Unsurprisingly no F.W. manager gave a positive interpretation of their greater resource loss.

This data is interesting on a number of grounds. Principally it presents the F.W. managers' interpretation of their greater loss: they were `ripped off'. This term strongly implies an element of being cheated of what was rightfully theirs and is based on past experience of resource allocation.

The interpretation of this greater loss relies on a perceived negative evaluation of some aspects of the F.W. division.

F.W. managers felt that they had suffered a loss of status, that the Director of the organisation was motivated by dislike of the F.W. division, and that their divisional leader was incompetent. These interpretations on the part of F.W. managers offer a further insight into the increased conflict with their leader, senior management, and R. and D.C.

Additionally the data shows that members will construct a number of explanations in the absence of a known priority, to explain an unacceptable situation and cope by rationalising it.

Summary

Managers interpreted their roles in expenditure reductions differently. These differences reflected particular management group sub-cultures. The terms-in-use for describing the management role were realism, responsibility, values, maturity, caring, emotionalism, and participation. Whilst those who co-operated were sure that their stance was right, those who resisted involvement were less sure. This uncertainty resulted from the number of constituents who were seen to influence management behaviour and the conflict between these. The co-operators were most influenced by senior management.

All managers reported an initial negative reaction to reductions, and an increase in intergroup conflict. Additionally F.W. managers noted changes: in their management team towards competition and disagreement; in their relationship with staff; in a move towards conflict with senior management; in an increase in senior management's control; and in a negative evaluation of various aspects of the F.W. division. Such changes were not noted by their R. and D.C. colleagues. The data on changes to management team practice is particularly notable because it indicates the two-way influence between reductions and group culture. Sub-culture influences responses to and interpretations of reductions; reductions can precipitate changes to this same culture, particularly when traditional values no longer guide behaviour, because these values no longer have utility.

7 Diagnosis through action: improving intergroup relations

Introduction

The purpose of this chapter is to describe and analyse an intervention and to evaluate it as a diagnostic tool. Whilst the intervention was designed to improve relations between two management groups - F.W.M.T. and R. and D.C.M.T. - which had worsened during stringency, it also provided useful diagnostic data about the differential effect of hard times on managerial sub-groups.

Firstly the role change from researcher to consultant is considered and then problem and strategy selection is examined. The stages of the intervention are noted, and the final intergroup meeting is considered in some detail. Data from this source is used diagnostically, to investigate the source of conflict, its effects on expenditure reductions, and to gain understanding of managerial sub-groups.

Role Change from Researcher to Consultant

Presenting, negotiating and conducting an intervention involves the practitioner in a change of presented role emphasis. The change is from one of eliciting or absorbing information, to actively initiating change in relation to a specific problem area. For the intervention to proceed, organisational members had to try to accept the legitimacy of this change despite the inherent ambiguities.

This was facilitated in three ways: creating an expectation of role change during data collection; members' evaluations of the conduct of data collection; and the commitment to the selected problem and action strategy. The first involved references to possible action outcomes whilst distancing myself from research outcomes on which action is less likely such as reports. In respect of the second as Brown (1972) points out:

> the subject of the investigator's study is simultaneously studying the investigator, and making decisions on the quantity and quality of the information he (or she) will provide (p. 698).

The process of data collection provides members with an evaluative measure of the researcher which is applied to any action recommended by that researcher. As the Deputy Director said:

> we wouldn't have let you (conduct in intervention) if we thought you'd bugger it up.

Finally the selected problem and solution strategy were acceptable. The F.W.M.T. leader said it was

> an excellent idea which hopefully will identify the real areas to concentrate on over the next six months.

The R. and D.C. leader was also agreeable, as he wanted

> a good working relationship with F.W.. It can't make matters worse.

Problem and Strategy Selection

Two major and connected problems were identified by managers: the hostile relationship between R. and D.C. and F.W. management teams in general, and, in particular, each group's management of expenditure reductions. The latter was seen to have influenced the former, producing what one senior manager observed as an 'all time low in interdivisional relations'. Both matters generated conflict but the former, whilst including reductions management, seemed to pose less of an initial threat to members, and was thus anticipated as less likely to produce the defensive reaction of rejection. Both topics were raised at individual, team and inter-team settings, but the problem of intergroup relations pre-dated that of reductions. The significance of good working relations, both for clients and for the organisation's non-service delivery activities, was acknowledged as was the fact that expenditure reductions had made intergroup relations worse.

The problem was processional rather than structural: intergroup contact as illustrated in Chapter 4 was being used by each group to reinforce and update information on the deficiencies of the other. It was also a forum for surfacing negative evaluations of one team by the other which impeded discussion of substantive matters. Structural change seemed an unlikely option in the short term due to resource scarcity, the recent restructuring of the R. and D.C. division, and the Director's reported opposition to structural change. The task was therefore to facilitate the workings of the existing structure.

An appropriate intervention would, it was believed, be one which exposed these processes, acknowledged them as a legitimate area for action, and enabled members to work through and find solutions to the problems. Though both expenditure reductions management and intergroup relations were areas of conflict, the latter seemed more likely to generate agreement on action between the parties. The Sherifs (1953) term this type of agreement, the discovery of a superordinate goal.

However, the advisability of addressing intergroup conflict is discussed in the literature on organisational development (O.D.) and if conflict is intense Bennis (1969: p. 45) regards attempts at resolution as inadvisable. He does not, however, define 'intense'. Earlier though, he refers to conflict resolution as an example of O.D. practice. Conflict in this case involved 'stereotyping and mutual distrust, if not downright hostility' (p. 4).

Henley (1975) suggests that action is inappropriate on issues which have a high salience for members, that is, where there is open conflict. Significance then, is attached to the level of conflict. Conversely, Schein (1985) states that:

> much of the work of organisational development practitioners deals with the knitting together of diverse and warring sub-cultures (p. 285)

Beckhard (1969) states that an operational goal of O.D. is to create conditions `where conflict is brought out and managed' rather than trying to `work around, or avoid, or cover up conflicts' (p. 14).

Intergroup conflict resolution is a major concern for both theorists and practitioners and the work of the Sherifs (1953) has made a major contribution to this field. They reviewed methods of reducing conflict between groups, from the use of rules or laws to regulate behaviour to the dissemination of information aimed at reducing stereotyping. Their experimental work with children identified the significance of superordinate goals, or mutually desired ends, as a means of fostering co-operation. They created competition between groups, then transformed this relationship to one of co-operation, through the introduction of a superordinate goals. To achieve the desired goal, competing groups had to co-operate and for the Sherifs, homogeneity of purpose was thus the key to intergroup co-operation.

In circumstances of conflict then, the consultant's job is to help the client identify areas where agreement on end states exists and help him use these to tackle conflict. Thus in determining whether action to resolve conflict is possible, it is important to identify possible superordinate goals.

The intervention focused on intergroup issues, as these were more easily and directly addressed than the management of stringency. In relation to the former, the parties were agreed that intergroup relations were poor and that conflict needed reducing. This was the superordinate goal, whereas in contrast, expenditure reductions were difficult to address as there was little agreement on either their nature or a clear end state. There was no easily identified superordinate goals.

An approach to improving intergroup relations is suggested by writers such as Blake et al (1964), Lorsch and Lawrence (1965), Merry and Allerhand (1977), Schein (1969), and Beckhard (1969). They use the conflict itself as the focus of intergroup discussions aimed at reducing it. This process is usually structured in the following way: the intragroup generation and intergroup sharing of stereotyped data by each group of the other leads to an identification and discussion of differences. Cross groups, comprising members of each group then consider solutions and the views elicited may be either perceptual (Blake et al: 1964; Schein: 1969) or evaluative (Fordyce and Weil: 1971; Merry and Allerhand: 1977). These studies indicated that interventions which address conflict can be productive. The intervention described here used the structure outlined above, and, following Blake et al and Schein, focused on the exchange of group perceptions in three categories: namely the group's view of itself, its view of the other group, and a prediction of the other group's view of it.

The intervention took place over a three-month period which provided flexibility by allowing more time to those management teams less familiar with such activities (R. and D.C.). Further, whilst F.W.M.T. took an hour to discuss the issue of their participating and to generate perceptions, R. and D.C.M.T. devoted four hours at two meetings to the task. This strategy also utilised the existing group and intergroup timetables of meetings, thus enabling the action to proceed without extra resources. Finally it seemed likely that any change would be more easily transferable to normal working life, if the intervention was perceived as `work' rather than `training'.

Implementation

The intervention involved a presentation to each management team leader, and then their respective teams. Each group produced its lists and these were then shared, discussed and clarified. Though it is not my purpose to analyse these' perspectives, they do provide a flavour of the intervention, and the basis for it. They are therefore set out in Appendix One. Specific problems on intergroup relations were identified at the first intergroup meeting, and in particular different responses to the management of expenditure reductions. Issues associated with expenditure reductions were considered at the second, and final, intergroup meeting.

Member responses to the first intergroup meeting were in the main positive and although one manager referred to the intervention as a `love-in' in a pejorative manner, comments such as `good', `useful', and `thank you'

153

were also made. Members expressed views to the group that: a trusting environment had been created; a climate of sharing was developing; that it was good going from ideas to practice; and that it was the first time such matters had been articulated.

On the basis of this development, it was agreed that a further meeting would be useful, to continue discussing intergroup problems and solutions. The most significant of these, expenditure reductions management, would be the focus. Though the community acknowledged that the action was incomplete, the second meeting resulted in a halt to the intervention and agreement to discuss the matter further was not acted on. Lack of time was given as a reason at one stage and apart from a brief meeting with the Deputy Director and request for a report some time later, (see Appendix Two), no further action was requested or taken on the matter.

The second meeting is analysed in detail, in respect of the perspective it provides on both the management of expenditure reductions, and on conflict.

The analysis of this falls into two parts; the first involved exchanges between F.W. and R. and D.C. managers: and the second, exchanges between F.W. managers and the senior manager who was both team leader of R. and D.C.M.T. and Deputy Director of the organisation. The analysis focuses on members' contributions, and interprets them with reference to the aim and immediate outcome of the intervention.

Part One

From the views expressed in the first part of the meeting, the nature of F.W. managers' problems with reductions management was highlighted, as was the degree of mutual understanding and concern. Conversely little was said in support, or condemnation, of the manager as bureaucrat - managers manage whatever the circumstances. The sympathetic acceptance of diversity in managerial circumstances, on the part of R. and D.C. managers, represented a success in terms of the goal of intergroup harmony. But this acceptance was also seen as a threat and as such was attacked in the second part of the meeting.

The terms in which F.W. managers' expressed their problems represented a significant change in emphasis succinctly expressed by a F.W. manager

> Senior management say we won't (manage expenditure reductions): we say we can't.

A value base and an operational base for action were identified and contrasted. Whereas prior to the intervention F.W. managers usually emphasised a value base in explaining their activities, during the interventions they emphasised an operational base. Thus one said

> I've no prescription for action; no one says what we've not got to provide,

whilst another said

> I've no solution.

Reference was made to value based opposition to reductions management - that is, the `will not' approach - but the bulk of F.W. managers' contributions concerned the operational - the `cannot' approach - and the difficulties they experienced. For example, they referred to contextual features such as pressure from opposing groups; the manager's need for the goodwill of his staff; and their union's unrealistic instruction not to manage.

One F.W. manager anticipated a discussion of expenditure reductions problems `might provide mutual support and understanding'. In response to F.W. managers' exploration of their problems, generally supportive statements were provided by R. and D.C. managers, such as

> we care what happens to F.W.

and this was in contrast to an attitude of indifference,

> O.K., F.W.'s down the Swannee;

155

an attitude which was for the most part rejected. Similarly a F.W. manager was concerned to protect the level of resources available to R. & D.C. managers

We are equally committed to no cuts in R. and D.C..

Mutual concern was the predominant feeling rather than indifference or competition.

The type of problems identified by F.W. managers were acknowledged by some of their R. & D.C. colleagues to be different and more difficult than those they faced managing expenditure reductions. For example, one R. & D.C. manager said that, unlike F.W.

R. & D.C. hasn't experienced the sharp end of expenditure reductions.... No posts have been lost.

There was, then, some acceptance that the management of reductions was adversely affected by the severity of the reductions being managed and that this applied to F.W. managers particularly because they were experiencing the `sharp end' in comparison with their R. and D.C. colleagues. The R. and D.C. manager mentioned above went on to say

We have it to go through,

`it' being the `sharp end' and loss of posts. One R. and D.C. manager also anticipated that he and his colleagues would in the future be presented with the type of management problems which F.W. managers were currently experiencing and describing.

Another response which in effect gave support to F.W. managers' definition of their problems, rather than dismissing or ignoring them, was by identification, or understanding, based on similarity of experience. One R. and D.C. manager acknowledged that she could identify with the issues raised by F.W. managers because she too had experienced some difficulty with reductions management. She perceived, for example, the beginnings of `a split with senior management'; had experienced conflicts with her staff; and had felt `isolated' both from those above and those below. She had also wondered `what to do: ignore or follow F.W.', for to follow F.W. meant resisting reductions; in the event she obeyed instructions. Her contribution was thus made in the light of an understanding gained from the experience of similar problems and from acknowledging rather than denying their reality.

Finally, F.W. managers were encouraged rather than discouraged to share their problems and `to tell you how I feel', as one F.W. manager said, by supportive, rather than undermining remarks from their R. and D.C. colleagues. For example,

It's useful to share the muddle.

It's the first time it's been shared at divisional level,

and

it's good sitting here hearing you feel sick.

One R. and D.C. manager however, said that

managers should manage,

that is, managers should operate as managers, whatever the circumstances. Interestingly, this statement reflected the perception of the management task by all R. and D.C.M.T. members when interviewed previously.

Attitudes on the part of the majority of R. and D.C. managers had by this time changed from a general condemnation of F.W. managers' activities, to one which was understanding of the effects of different circumstances. There was also an identification with similar experiences and an expressed sympathy for, and interest in, those in a worse position. Similarly F.W. managers expressed concern for the resources available to their R. and D.C. colleagues, couched their contributions in terms of operational difficulties, and refrained from condemning the alternative management strategy of their R. and D.C. colleagues. The extent of the change can be measured by comparing the comments reported here, with the interview data interpreting their roles as managers as set out in Chapter 6.

Why these changes in attitude occurred is difficult to analyse, because of the potentially large number of influencing variables. In part they stem from F.W. managers' greater experience of managing reductions, and, in the case of R. and D.C. managers, with the anticipation of more reductions to come. The atmosphere of trust built up during the first exercise assisted in the discussion of these changes and the second meeting of the intervention provided a forum within which these altered views could be legitimately expressed.

Different response to expenditure reductions can inhibit rather than encourage intergroup co-operation especially, for example, meetings to recommend specific reductions. The intervention demonstrated that this tendency may be reduced where, after some catharsis, views can be expressed in managerial problem-solving terms.

Part Two

In Part Two of the meeting the direction and tone of the discussion were changed, by the senior manager in charge of R. and D.C.M.T., in a largely successful attempt to reverse the understanding generated earlier. He did this by rejecting F.W. managers' definitions of their problems using a two-pronged attack: that their contributions had been `dishonest' and `value-based'; and that they had on another recent occasion `acted in bad faith' on the issue of reductions management.

Part Two of the meeting began when the management team leaders were asked to contribute, and whilst the F.W. team leader said nothing, the R. and D.C. team leader said:

masturbation is not a spectator sport.

This led to heated, acrimonious and lengthy exchange between the latter and some F.W. managers about their contribution to the session and their involvement of the union in negotiations to manage reductions. In respect of the latter issue, subsequent exchanges revealed that some F.W. managers may have agreed with some senior managers on means of managing reductions and that this agreement had been rescinded by the F.W. managers' union. The focus of the meeting changed from a horizontal relationship between the two middle management teams, to a hierarchical one between F.W. managers and senior management. From being reasonably open and constructive, contributions became competitive.

The R. and D.C. team leader subsequently accepted his role in re-directing the focus of the meeting; he

> threw the meeting off course; it was one of the few occasions when I allowed myself the luxury of saying what I thought. The subject was around and would have come out, whatever.

It is doubtful if this was so, for the subject of F.W. managers' bad faith `came out' because he introduced it and the attacking style in which he spoke ensured defensive responses. The subject was referred to indirectly at the beginning of the meeting:

> something has happened which F.W. is still coming to terms with.

What this something was, was not however pursued.

It was re-introduced only after the exchanges in Part One of the meeting had taken place; that is, after members of the R. and D.C.M.T. expressed understanding of, and sympathy for, their F.W. colleagues' predicament. This partially explains the R. and D.C. team leader's re-introduction of the subject in such a dramatic fashion. His contribution was designed to be inflammatory and attacking from his style of delivery, the terms used, the volume of his voice, and the content. His behaviour was unusual in comparison with that in other settings where he operated in a calm but directing fashion, but on this occasion he allowed himself not only the luxury of saying what he thought, but also the luxury of saying this in a provocative manner. This combination of content and style increased the likelihood of defensive responses from F.W. managers.

The options open to him at the end of Part One of the intervention are as follows. He could, for example, have remained silent, as did his peer senior manager (the F.W.M.T. leader), though this would not have been `in character'; he could have followed his team members in expressing understanding of F.W. managers' more difficult position; or he could have focused on particular problems raised and suggested solutions. In the event

159

he condemned F.W. managers' contributions to the meeting, and their activities generally. An attempt to explain this behaviour now follows.

The status of the contributor, and the nature of his contribution, both in its dramatic form and content, encouraged an observing role by those managers not directly involved in the discussion between F.W. managers and senior managers. Perhaps they preferred not to be involved in overt conflict, thus not attracting to themselves the anger that was present at the meeting.

My role reverted to that of the observer for my initial surprise was replaced by a consideration of alternative actions. None however seemed appropriate. I concluded that the spell had been broken, that the work on intergroup harmony had been nullified, and that I had lost control of the intervention. Nevertheless there was some interest in the group in pursuing this new topic and I had an objective in collecting further data.

Those managers who were directly involved wished to resolve matters and the senior manager clearly felt angry about what he perceived had happened. F.W. managers responded to, rather than ignored, his attack, being variously concerned to clarify what had happened, to distance themselves from it, or to justify their action. They also defended their contribution to Part One of the meeting. For a variety of reasons then, both parties to the exchange had an interest in pursuing the issue once it had been raised.

The senior manager had another concern resulting from Part One of the meeting. He perceived the outcomes as a threat to the bureaucratic perspective on the middle manager's job. This view of the manager's role which was shared by other senior managers had received scant attention or support until he spoke. In contrast, a statement which articulated different and more difficult circumstances had received an understanding and sympathetic response from his own management team. He undoubtedly noted that some of his managers would, as one of them implied, have difficulties managing, when experiencing the `sharp end' of reductions. They would not in these circumstances necessarily act as they had done in the past, that is `follow orders', but might instead `follow F.W'.

He therefore vigorously defended his position, as he had in the past, and attempted to re-impose it on the group. He did this by denying the validity of an approach which took into account differences in the severity of reductions and related managerial circumstances, rather than pointing to any solution that had been arrived at during his discussion with F.W. managers.

At the same time he used pre-meeting events as a justification for rejecting the validity of F.W. managers' contributions which were, he stated, both self-indulgent and dishonest. By denying the operational reality of what F.W. managers' were saying, he also undermined the understanding response they had received from members of his own management team.

The effect of his intervention was an avoidance of the problems and solutions associated with the F.W. managers' task, and instead this group were re-cast in the role of managerial villains. Conversely the heroes were those who continued to respond in a `managerial manner' to the issue of financial reductions. A clear message was thus given to his own management team to either continue to manage or be cast as a villain.

The positive outcomes of the intervention were dissipated and conflict between the two teams encouraged, for rather than accepting diversity between the two middle management teams, uniformity was re-asserted as the only legitimate reality and an indication given of the strength of opposition which deviance would attract. Consideration is now given to the source and results of the conflict evident in this event.

Conflict Resolution and Superordinate Goals

Earlier in this chapter the literature was examined to ascertain appropriate responses to organisational conflict. It now seems that significance needs to be attached to discovering superordinate goals, which determine how far any intervention is likely to succeed in resolving the conflict, whatever the level of conflict may be. There was agreement between both parties - R. and D.C.M.T. and F.W.M.T. - that the conflict between them needed to be resolved and relationships improved. On the basis of this superordinate goal the intervention proceeded successfully which suggests that it is the existence of such goals rather than the level of conflict itself that is most significant in forecasting the effectiveness of an intervention. Overt conflict for example, where matched by a high level of agreement on superordinate goals, can be effectively resolved.

Action should not be ruled out though, where agreement is at a low level, or superordinate goals are elusive, as appeared to be the case with F.W. managers and senior management. The intervention strategy in these circumstances is best focused on delineating areas of disagreement, and defining mechanisms for reaching compromise, such as role negotiation. This was recommended in my report to the organisation (see Appendix Two).

The intervention was not intended to improve relations between senior management and F.W. managers, though the need for this was revealed in the course of the work. The extent to which these two groups shared a superordinate goal in respect of expenditure reductions is not known. That they met in another setting to discuss the issue suggests some measure of agreement on the need to manage expenditure reductions, and indeed one party to the meeting believed agreement had been reached. In view of his contribution it seems the developments between the two middle management teams were perceived as a threat by the senior manager who took steps to reverse them. The nature of this threat is explored in the following section.

Rationales for Management Action

The basis of the conflict about managing expenditure reductions revealed by contributions made during the intervention reported above was the differing perceptions of the rationale for managerial action. These differences are represented diagrammatically along two axes:

Axis 1: Value rationale for action

`will' ←------------------------------→ `will not'

Action reflects personal, professional or political values.

Axis 2: Operational rationale for action

`can' ←------------------------------→ `cannot'

Action depends on contextual features.

The nature of these features and the extent to which they are present determines how far management decisions about reductions can be operationalised. Combining these two axes produces Figure 3.

FIGURE 3
PERCEPTIONS OF ACTION

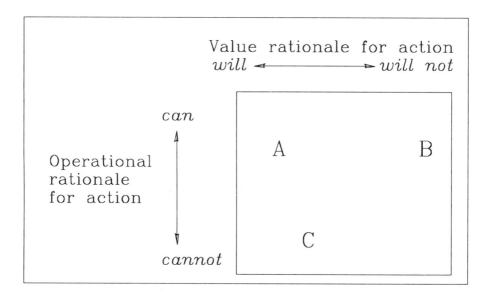

Points A, B and C above represent the following positions:

Point A:

Managers are able and willing to act, whatever the circumstances: the `managers should manage' view. This ideal was, and remained the view held by senior management, and by R. and D.C. managers until the intervention.

Point B:

Managers `can' manage, but `will not'. This remained the senior management perspective on F.W. Managers' behaviour. It was the initial view of F.W. managers by their R. and D.C. colleagues and by F.W. managers of themselves.

Point C:

Managers are willing to act, and put aside their values to some extent, were it not for unresolved operational problems. This perspective was emphasised by F.W. Managers during the intervention, and was one which R. and D.C. managers subscribed to, in contrast to their team leader.

The changes in perceptions can be analysed as follows. There was a retreat from strong, value-based perceptions and a movement towards an emphasis on expedient action by both management teams. There was also movement towards some measure of agreement between the groups. Neither of these changes applied to the senior manager whose views went unchallenged by his fellow senior manager and whose contribution to the intervention was examined above.

The substance of the conflict, and the extent of the differences between F.W. managers and senior management is apparent in that the former argued in terms of operating, the latter in terms of values. They were thus not in dispute about degrees of difference on the same matter, but about two different interpretative schemes.

At the senior management level, value differences were an acceptable explanation of different responses, whilst differences in contextual features were not. With this view of reality, little difference is perceived between the circumstances of different management teams other than those of values. Whilst values were used to interpret the behaviour of others, their use as a basis for action by these others is dismissed as being in some way self-indulgent and inappropriate. On the other hand, any acknowledgement of operational difficulties raises more serious issues, such as the way a manager deals with opposition from his or her staff. Such issues require a more sophisticated problem definition and solution strategy to take into account and deal with differences in contextual features. There were clear value differences between the management teams, but an explanation based on value differences alone represents an incomplete definition of their problems when facing hard decisions on cutbacks.

During the course of data collection operational difficulties were infrequently identified as the basis of differing managerial behaviour. The intervention revealed the significance of such operational difficulties, and thus shifted the emphasis away from a totally value-based rationale for action.

Summary

An account of the consulting intervention is provided in this chapter, and the data produced from it is analysed as a diagnostic device to help understand aspects of the management of stringency. The significance of agreement on superordinate goals rather than the overall level of conflict was found to be important in predicting the success of intergroup interventions. In the particular instance outlined above, movement towards horizontal intergroup harmony was facilitated, though this harmony was perceived as a threat and attacked as such by senior management.

Two rationales for management action, `value' and `operational', were distinguished, and conflicts between them examined. Whilst values were an acceptable and easily dismissable explanation of behaviour, operational difficulties were not. A solely value-based explanation of managerial decision-making represents an incomplete analysis. A move from a value to an operationally based explanation of reductions management was detailed. The significance of sub-cultural values and operating context in the effective management of stringency is examined in more detail in the following chapter.

8 Organisational monetarism in practice

Introduction

This chapter analyses the concept of organisational monetarism introduced in Chapter 3, and examines three of the five assumptions on which it is based, using data derived from the organisation's middle management teams. These three assumptions are: an interest in financial management and cost effectiveness; the ability to specify, and thereby quantify, task and outcomes; and the causal link between financial stringency and innovative behaviour which leads to enhanced organisational effectiveness.

The concept is shown to be deficient as a predictive device because it does not take into account group sub-cultures and contextual features such as stage of development and unionateness. These are features peculiar to the internal environment in which different groups operate. These features pre-date the advent of stringency and influence members' responses to expenditure reductions. These influences are more powerful than a behavioural imperative towards innovation which is inherent in the concept of organisational monetarism. Pre-existing features of managers' situations are more significant because they influence the extent to which managers can manage reductions; that is, they determine the ease or difficulty with which the values and practice associated with reductions are assimilated by the group.

A number of authors refer to the significance of pre-existing organisational features in determining responses to expenditure reductions. Thus Whetton (1981) refers to

deeply entrenched organisational dynamics (p. 91)

in educational institutions; Jick and Murray (1982) identify personality, environmental information networks and internal design as significant in determining

preparedness for potential crisis events such as funding cut-backs (p. 163).

Rubin (1980) identifies strong leadership and budget flexibility as essential, otherwise

retrenchment cannot be carried out (p. 175).

Nottenburg and Fedor (1983) focus on an organisation's pre-existing myth system as a means of interpreting responses to reductions. The following analysis introduces some additional features which affect reductions management, and examines these at group rather than organisational level. This focus on pre-existing organisational features as a means of analysing responses to expenditure reductions suggests that these be added to the model `of basic elements in the response to organisational decline' which Murray and Jick (1985: p. 113) propose.

The analysis of members' responses is focused on `being able to' as well as `wanting to' manage reductions, using distinctions made by Scott (1976) which were reflected in the intervention described in Chapter 7. Rather than relying primarily on personal and political values of group sub-culture as an explanation, the analysis is widened to include the influence of other features, especially the extent to which financial control was seen as a significant factor in group sub-culture.

The Significance of Finance

Much of the work on expenditure reductions often assumes that the problem is essentially financial, although this is not always apparent in practice. Finance is defined here as a concern with and commitment to budgetary control. A focus on financial matters at the time of reductions was apparent to organisational managers. The F.W. team leader, who had just begun work with the department when stringency became an issue, said

> since I joined, I've been pre-occupied with the financial side
> of things.

A number of F.W. managers remarked, with little enthusiasm, that finance was necessarily beginning to play a larger part in organisational life. The terms in which expenditure reductions were presented to managers (Chapters 3 and 5) were those of budgetary and financial control, and the solution to financial stringency appeared to lie in financial measures.

Reactions to reductions appear to be, in part, a result of a group's response to this financial emphasis and the extent to which the group's sub-culture includes the values and practices of financial management and control. R and D.C.M.T. had methods for and experience of financial management, whilst F.W.M.T. did not.

Financial Practice

Unlike their R. and D.C. colleagues, F.W. managers did not keep a regular check of spending during the year. Their team leader explained this as follows:

> Monthly spending figures and projections have gone to pot
> in the current crisis. The normal methods of financial
> management became irrelevant.

A team member said they had `never done so', and the F.W.M.T. leader's recommendation to his team to keep a regular check of spending supports the latter version of F.W. managerial practice. Control measures already in

168

existence in R. and D.C.M.T. were thus recommended for introduction. In R. and D.C.M.T. financial control was a matter of course. As one member said:

we try to pick up the resource position before it's too late

to keep abreast of consumption to prevent overspending. F.W.M.T. did not consider spending patterns at any of their meetings. One group thus had a tradition of financial management, a system of budgetary control and experience of operating it, whereas the other did not.

F.W. managers in contrast to R. and D.C. managers experienced difficulty allocating resources internally. When one R. and D.C. manager overspent by five thousand pounds, another manager found the sum from his own budget. Because they found it difficult to agree, F.W.M.T. spent some time deciding how home-help, and overtime hours were to be divided amongst them, and referred to these protracted discussions as indicating a lack of expertise in resource allocation. Unlike their R. and D.C. colleagues, individual F.W. managers did not have separate budgets for some spending areas, for example, fostering. Budgets were joint ones between team members. Ideally there was a corporate approach to consumption, and agreement and trust were important in ensuring an acceptable and fair distribution of jointly held resources. All R. and D.C. managers were responsible for budgetary control in their sub-units, whereas in F.W. the team leader had the responsibility for budgetary control of all members of his group.

Different Group Attitudes to Financial Management

The two middle management teams were seen to have different attitudes to finance. A senior manager said

R. and D.C.M.T. have a more positive attitude to finance and budget control whereas some F.W. managers think it's irrelevant.

There was, said their leader, and in contrast to F.W.M.T.

a bigger financial component in R. and D.C.M.T.

in relation to the management task. An R. and D.C. middle manager said that `budgetary control' was an area where R. and D.C. differed from F.W.; he suggested this was because

> R. and D.C. have an enormous one (budget to control), F.W. don't even have buildings.

F.W. managers' attitude to financial management was noted by their leader when he speculated about devolving responsibility for financial control to team members. He expected a negative response and remarked to his D.M.T. colleagues that F.W.M.T. `will lynch me'. Though he was not lynched, his offer was not accepted by team members on the grounds of lack of manpower, lack of skills, lack of interest, timing (it was said by one member to be `a funny time' to introduce the issue), and a perception of the management role which excluded financial management.

Lack of Skill

F.W.M.T. perceived themselves as financially unskilled for, as one member put it, they were

> naive about money; until recently I had no idea of cost.

Another referred to their `innocence' in this respect. Yet another felt that

> if we take on the job, there'll be more emphasis on and we'll be more closely involved in money and finance. We need training in budgetary control,

and he referred to `complex new skills' which

> are more difficult to learn-as-we-go in a time of stringency as there's little room for manoeuvre.

These views were expressed at a team meeting and were supported by comments made privately. For example, one member said the group was

> financially weak and incompetent

and in view of their lack of skill they would have difficulty in managing tasks with a financial component competently. A number of authors recognise that the extent to which a group can deal with the requirements of a new situation depends in part on their skills in relation to these requirements. Thus, in writing of reductions management in educational institutions, Yarmolinksy (1975) remarked that

> faculty are spectacularly lacking in the analytic tools necessary to work out major programme changes (p. 63).

Cyert (1975) agrees, and recommends training in the

> underlying discipline of resource allocation skills (p. 11).

Differences in Interest in Financial Management

There were various views on the relevance of finance within the F.W.M.T. but the majority of members did not appear to be very interested. An extreme view was that

> finance and estimates are the last thing I'm interested in,

whilst another manager said

> finance is not given much weight, I try to remember but I forget.

Initially it may appear that a psychological model, utilising concepts such as denial and avoidance, or Fink et al's (1971) notion of defensive retreat, would be useful in analysing this data. Such concepts would help to explain the

171

above attitudes as avoidance mechanisms for coping with the unacceptable. However, a more productive analysis may be derived from two alternative concepts: experience and opposition. Lack of interest and/or competence was firstly linked to the groups' past experience of resource plenty, and secondly to an opposition which was drawn between professionally and financially based decisions.

Past Experience of Resource Management

In the past F.W.M.T. enjoyed an abundance of resources; they `had massive resources'. A senior manager remarked that until recently F.W.M.T. had enjoyed the `lion's share' and `endless' departmental resources; on the other hand R. and D.C. were the `poor relations'; they were `starved of resources'. There was no external control from councillors and one F.W. manager said

> the message in the past has been: `spend as much as you like; to hell with limits; the Council will pay up.'

Another said

> for some time there have been few limits, there's been a lot of money around. It was easy to get a video and a reel to reel tape. I'd said I wanted one or the other but they said there's enough for both. The Council encouraged overspending, 30%, 40%; there were no complaints, overspending was regarded as a success.

Overspending was justified on the basis of Council policy:

> some areas have always been overspent because of the Council's policy on waiting lists,

and

> fostering and agency placements have never been subject to control.

172

Budgetary control was then a foreign concept to F.W. managers who had had the experience of resource abundance; few, or no controls on overspending; and the expectation of more money if they did. As their team leader put it

> F.W.M.T. is used to making difficult decisions with individual cases not with resources.

The influence of the past is used by a number of authors, for example Scott (1974), Green (1974), Boulding (1975), Whetton (1980:a and b), and Jick and Murray (1982), to account for the absence of a theory and practice of managing resource stringency. For example, Whetton (1980:a) makes a point that

> organisational theories and research accurately reflect prevailing organisational reality (p. 579).

There has been organisational decline during the period of general growth, which Glassberg (1978) refers to as the

> generally rising pattern of public expenditure (p. 325).

but as Scott (1976) and Levine (1978) point out, this has been regarded as anomalous or as periods of consolidation. Decline management has not permeated the mainstream of organisational theory and practice.

Because research has been carried out in organisations that were expanding and this was the norm, the problems highlighted were those which related to, or resulted from growth. Boulding (1975) believes that

> at a practical level our institutions and ways of thinking have survived because they were adapted to an age of rapid growth (p. 8).

As a corollary to this, some authors point out that the theory and practice which developed during this period is inappropriate to standstill or decline. For example Perry (1972) and Scott (1974) suggest systems theory, which ascribes decline to old age or malfunctioning, is unable to explain decline due to financial stringency. Perhaps the most serious problem

173

is that many skills that were highly desirable during the last thirty years may well not be needed in the next thirty years (Boulding: 1975: p. 8).

Similarly a number of authors refer to organisational development techniques, particularly those which concern managing change and fostering co-operation, as being predicated on the availability of slack resources. In the absence of slack resources, such practices it is argued, (for example Levine: 1978, and Whetton: 1980:a and b) become less relevant, and consensus building solutions of the win/win variety which are feasible in abundant times, are often no longer possible in stringency, when one organisational group can only win at the expense of another. This, though, is not invariably the case, as the intervention described in the previous chapter indicates. Generally, the literature suggests that previous experience of management growth cannot simply be reversed in decline but that new skills are needed.

Conflict between 'Financial' or 'Professional' Decisions

F.W. managers' views of financial management are also revealed by the perceived conflict between decisions based on professional as opposed to financial criteria. F.W. managers said

> people in the area should not be guided by costs, but what is best for the kids;
>
> Professional judgements cannot be related to money but how it feels;
>
> Money and efficiency terms are not appropriate for some decisions.

Another F.W. manager drew a distinction between 'professional decisions' and 'the rules of finance and accounting', from which it appeared that a professional decision was one which excluded any financial element. This nicely illustrates the difference between formal and substantive rationalities noted by Weber (1968): the latter, substantive rationality, may consider the purely formal rationality of calculating in monetary terms as of quite secondary importance or even as fundamentally inimicable to their respective ultimate ends (p. 86).

The distinction between professional and financial values is also noted by Webb (1979):

Professional values have allowed and do allow many field-workers to divorce `professional' decisions from considerations of resource allocation. The commitment to meet needs does not readily recognise resource questions as pertinent or legitimate (p. 102).

There was also present an unstated fear that the financial element might become the overriding criteria for decisions on client care. One F.W. manager complained that with stringency,

we're constantly justifying decisions in financial terms.

This fear is noted by a number of authors including Cheit (1971). Wilburn and Worman (1980) term this efficiency mongering: to save money regardless of the effects on performance.

F.W. managers were not alone in being uninterested and unfamiliar with financial management matters, or in perceiving conflict between professionally based and financially based decisions. Some authors recognise that their prescriptions for managing reductions may not meet with an enthusiastic welcome, because of the unfamiliarity of the concepts which underlie their prescriptions and the way in which such concepts are valued. Concepts such as `finance' and `productivity' are often seen as being in opposition to professional goals. For example Cyert (1978) in relation to managing universities of constant or decreasing size maintains that

in addition, financial criteria must be given a heavy weight in developing criteria for eliminating activities, and such an emphasis is contrary to academic thinking (p. 344).

Cazalis (1979), in the context of managing austerity in the university sector, qualifies his suggestion of introducing cost control and productivity concepts by pointing out that these are foreign, suspect and seen as irrelevant by the teaching profession.

They seem to be taboo, on the grounds that productivity, for example, conflicts with quality and creativity (p. 41).

The hardest job, he suggests, will be the introduction of these concepts and convincing others of their relevance, but he does not offer solutions. Judge (1978) too points out that

efficiency has not been the most familiar concept in the vocabulary of personal social services in recent years (p. 153).

Cheit (1973) makes a similar point, believing that concepts such as budget plans and control devices were regarded as

satisfying some remote bureaucratic requirement (p. 60).

Yet both Schatz (1975) and Schick (1978) point to the importance of financial management concepts being `accepted' or `internalised' if they are to be effective, and Schatz (1975) reports that

failure to seek acceptance (from those involved) often leads to failure of financial management devices (p. 130).

Changes in technique need the approval of those affected, and this has to be actively pursued, rather than assumed. For Schick (1978) internalisation

where doing it (financial control) the proper way is accepted as a routine matter (p. 515)

is significant for the practice of financial control. A major stumbling block to the adoption of organisational monetarism is the level of familiarity and legitimacy which such concepts are seen to have within the worlds to which they are introduced.

In the case of R. and D.C.M.T., for example, financial control was already part of their group's sub-culture, whereas F.W.M.T. regarded financial management as uninteresting, interfering with their professional practice, and (based on their experience in more plentiful times) of no concern to them.

The less familiar such concepts are, the less they are regarded as relevant, and the less likely they are to be accepted or acted upon. Unfamiliarity results in perceived irrelevance, in disinclination and rejection. This suggests that responses to stringency are based on grounds additional to personal and political values, such as how the group views and manages the financial element in the manager's role. The assumption of organisational monetarism, that financial management is familiar and legitimate, was not supported by the behaviour of the F.W.M.T.

Pattern of Spending

Some managers linked the ease or difficulty with which reductions were managed by the two middle management teams to the type of resource managed by each team. For example, the R. and D.C. team leader maintained that reductions were

> emotional in F.W. as it's mainly people: most money goes on salaries and to save money you have to leave these vacancies open.

Hill (1979) confirms this by maintaining that social work `time' is the main resource controlled by F.W. On the other hand, R. and D.C. as an establishment based service, spent money on the upkeep of these establishments. An R. and D.C. manager was thus able to recommend reductions in for example, garden maintenance, which was something which he referred to as non-essential. It was suggested by F.W. Managers that it is easier to reduce spending which does not involve staff who deliver a professional service.

Size of Reductions

Given the significance placed on the size of reductions in analysing managerial responses at the macro-organisational level, (Murray and Jick: 1985; Gill and Pratt: 1986) the relevance of this variable in relation to the managers at the micro-level is considered. Size in the abstract, divorced from managers' meanings was not significant, whereas size of reductions as an evaluative and comparative device was.

Size of reductions was used by a minority of managers who co-operated to justify their actions, and criticise the response of F.W. colleagues. Reference was made to the level of reductions not being high enough to warrant resistance activity: these managers made a judgment about the level of cuts above which they would cease to co-operate. Chapters 6 and 7 made clear that current reductions were not seen to have breached the limit, which was not specified in monetary terms, but in terms of their effects, such as closing homes. When this limit was reached it was implicit that action, such as resistance in various forms, would be considered.

Interestingly, R. and D.C. managers followed instructions to draw up recommendations in their division over and above the minimum required by the Council, and did so without difficulty. One manager proposed closing his section down altogether. Given this group's management role was largely defined by supervisors, it seems likely they would have co-operated with reductions of significantly increased size and would only consider forms of resistance if reductions were major and led, for example, to all homes being closed. For an establishment based division such a result would clearly involve radical restructuring.

F.W. managers, on the other hand, objected to the instructions to recommend reductions and manage their effects. It was the reductions of expenditure rather than the size of these, that was significant, and opposition was expressed in these terms. F.W.M.T. continued to oppose reductions, though in a different form, even after councillors had increased their resources; thus an increase in resources did not lead to co-operation but continued opposition in the form of withdrawal. It is not therefore possible to causally connect size of reduction with managerial response. The effect of differential reductions is now considered.

In Chapter 6 we saw that F.W. managers interpreted `losing more' resources as reflecting a negative evaluation of their work and their behaviour by decision makers. This resulted in a negative evaluation of the managers' skill in obtaining resources through `blaming' and `scapegoating'.

Size of reductions was used to compare the resultant task of managers who received more or less resources; there was a recognition during the intervention described in the previous chapter that greater cuts resulted in a more difficult management task. Greater reductions as a spur to innovation was not raised at any point.

The size of reductions was referred to indirectly and comparatively - `more' and `less', `better' and `worse' - rather than by reference to specific sums, such as percentages of total spending. Comparisons were made publicly and privately with the past when there was an absence of stringency, with future expectations, and with the allocation of the other division. Indeed it appears that the absolute size of cuts stated in particular sums and percentages were less significant to members than comparative amounts between divisions.

Thus size of reduction was interpreted and utilised as an evaluative device. Differential reductions resulted in a more or less difficult management task, and were referred to in comparative not absolute terms. Size of reductions was seldom referred to as a rationale for action.

Differences in Team Tasks

A minority of managers mentioned the extent to which divisional tasks were specifiable and tangible, and the effect this had on the management of stringency. In this case there was some support for the view that there were differences between F.W. and R. and D.C. in respect of environmental pressures and task outcome specificity. F.W. operated a community based, generic and universal service, whilst R. and D.C. was establishment based, providing primarily physical care services to specific, selected and restricted client groups. Aspects of these differences are considered below.

Differences in Environmental Control

The F.W. M.T. were less favourably positioned to control their environment than their R. and D.C. colleagues as F.W. occupied a boundary position with the client environment: what Hill (1979) termed the `Social Services Department's front line' (p. 116). They dealt primarily with client-presented problems and in addition, performed a client filtering service for R. and D.C.. Clients made initial contact with the F.W. division, and were then passed on to R. and D.C. if the matter could not be resolved. Whilst neither group could predict the number of clients requiring help, a finite number of places in establishments were available and limits were imposed by R. and D.C.. F.W. were not able to define such limits so readily, and in any event did not consider it to be professionally appropriate. R. and D.C. then exerted more control over their client environment than their F.W. colleagues.

Differences in Task Specificity

F.W. were less easily able and committed than R. and D.C. to specifying their goals and usually defined them in very general terms such as meeting unmet needs. They showed a distinct lack of enthusiasm for defining the task in any detail, and the mention of goal setting provoked a majority response of `Oh God, not that'. R. and D.C.'s task of providing physical care to specific client groups was necessarily less diffuse. As an R. and D.C. manager said

> For F.W. it is difficult to point to what they're doing whereas R. and D.C. have bodies (clients in care) and bricks and mortar (establishments). If it's a choice between a higher vacancy element in F.W. or closing a home, I know which they (councillors) would choose.

Because one group could point to tangible and easily quantifiable evidence of their activities they were better protected from the imposition of reductions by those who had to decide between the tangible and the intangible. The F.W. team leader suggested that a vague task was ripe for reductions (`community work: a vague area - ideal for cuts'). In this way members linked task clarity and justification of resources consumption: the more tangible a task was, the more justifiable it became and the less vulnerable to cuts.

F.W. could less easily point to the results of their activities in relation to resource consumption than R. and D.C. The latter could refer to `bodies' or people in care, as a visible and quantifiable result or outcome. They could point to the buildings themselves as a product of their spending, and did`so by regularly showing councillors round them. On the other hand, the clients of F.W. were out in the community and `results' were less easy to specify, particularly in supportive and preventative work. For example, that a social work intervention prevented a non-accidental injury (child battering) is difficult to substantiate or quantify. This might account for F.W. managers' reaction to the quantification of results. In the words of their team leader:

> F.W. has no review, no criteria, no success measurement. Any questioning of these areas (fostering, community work), provokes an almost Pavlovian response: it's seen as an attack. There's no question, the attitude is it's here, it's good and it stays.

Judge (1978) makes the same point:

> any attempt to measure, define or even comment on its (social work) effectiveness is usually open to everything from cautious qualification to instant hostility (p. 175),

but, as he also points out, such a process of definition and measurement is necessary to

> demonstrate productive efficiency (p. 175).

The nature of social work was ill defined as professional social work skills such as counselling and support are difficult to quantify and present in terms which readily demonstrate their effectiveness.

Additionally R. and D.C. could justifiably claim to be working to capacity should their establishments be full, but no similar limit could so easily be placed on the number of clients F.W. could be expected to deal with. Accepting the benefits of F.W.'s activities involved a greater element of trust on the part of decision makers than was the case with R. and D.C.'s work.

181

The ability to specify criteria and show results from divisional tasks is of assistance in managing reductions for it facilitates decision making by managers who have to make hard choices. It provides a justification for spending and for the protection of an area of work. Conversely, it seems that the less easy to specify tasks and outcomes are, the more vulnerable they are to reductions.

Ease of Measurement

One of the assumptions of organisational monetarism with its emphasis on financial management is that quantification and measurement is unproblematic and objective. Authors such as Bogue (1972), Balderstone (1972), Cyert (1975 and 1978), Self (1980), and Sizer (1981) have all stressed the importance of developing performance measures of tasks in stringent times. However, they recognise that there are difficulties. So for example, Cyert (1975), whilst stressing the importance of quantifiable methods of evaluating sub-units, confesses that

> the difficulty lies in defining quality of performance. (p. 9)

Hamblin and Adams (1983) attempted to develop criteria of supervisory effectiveness in the public and private sector; they concluded

> there was little or no agreement amongst managers and supervisors on how (if at all) supervisory effectiveness could be assessed (p. 31).

They point to the

> difficulty inherent in trying to define and measure what is meant by the terms effectiveness and efficiency (p. 21).

Balderstone (1972) too raises the many serious problems of measuring and interpreting the quality and quantity of educational input and, as he says

not much progress has been made in measuring educational
output or educational quality (p. 24).

This stems from the difficulty mentioned by authors such as Frances and
Stone (1956), Bogue (1972), Ginsberg (1975), Mitnick (1978), Starbuck et al
(1978), and Bozeman and Slusher (1979), that it is less easy to quantify
information which is variously characterised as subtle, diffuse, subjective,
less tangible, qualitative or indirect, and such information may therefore be
ignored. For example Gill (1981) suggests that

> easily quantifiable goals may become primary goals and
> those which are more difficult to specify may become
> secondary (p. 8),

and Ullman (1975) states that

> we can count bodies but we cannot readily measure the
> quality of what they know (p. 145).

Thus, whilst performance measures are necessary in stringent times, the
difficulty inherent in measuring qualitative tasks results in an emphasis on
those which are more readily quantifiable.

Having examined how the two management groups were
differentially affected by the sub-cultural feature of financial management,
and the contextual features of environmental control, task visibility and
measurement, two further contextual features are now considered: stage of
professional development, and unionateness.

Stage of Professional Development

F.W. was recognised as being at a more advanced stage of professional
development than R. and D.C. in that they had a longer professional history
and more expertise. A function of development is the creation of awareness
of what should be provided, and how this should be achieved. This
awareness will be higher within a developed service. Reducing such a service
in strict times will present a greater problem for managers as there will be

expectations of further development and growth. A group which is more professionally developed will experience greater difficulty in reconciling professional standards with resource reductions.

Unionateness

F.W. and R. and D.C. were also differentiated by unionateness. F.W. was highly unionised, whilst R. and D.C. was not. Management of reductions was more difficult for F.W. managers because union instructions operated in the F.W. division in three respects. Managers were faced with managing a resistant and cohesive workforce who, for example, refused to cover work left undone when vacancies were left unfilled. Managers were union members themselves, and were bound by union instructions, though the nature of these was disputed; in effect these instructions inhibited their involvement in the reductions management delegated by senior management. Finally staff loyalty and co-operation, and managers' legitimacy in the eyes of staff was seen to depend on managers following the union line. (These matters were referred to in detail in Chapter 6). For R. and D.C. none of this applied: levels of unionateness amongst staff and managers were low, and thus the union's instructions had no significant effect.

The inhibiting effect of union activity is noted by Levine et al (1981). They identify `public service unions' (p 626), as one of three institutional actors in the management of local government resource decline and point to the level of union activity, which they term politicisation, as being one of the two significant features in assisting or inhibiting decline management. The other feature is centralised control. Union activity, they tell us, inhibits cutback management by reducing the administrator's power to act. McTighe (1979) also refers to the union as being an influential actor in the management of decline.

Task Operationalisation

Not all managers then were able to operationalise the reductions task with the same degree of ease. Because of the differential effects of the organisational factors outlined above, some managers found the tasks of reductions more problematic. A number of managers said that if R. and D.C.M.T. can do it (manage reductions) why cannot F.W.M.T.. This implied that both groups were in the same position and that F.W.M.T. could manage reductions if it wanted to, but was not motivated to do so.

Scott (1976) makes the same distinction between `wanting to' and `being able to', and asks rhetorically

> Can management deal with decline ....of course it can. The issue is not being unable to deal with decline, but wanting to deal with it (p. 56).

This chapter and the previous one has made clear that certain practical factors are influential in determining participation in or ability to manage stringency and these are over and above personal and political values.

Though personal and political values were the more popular explanation of management behaviour, it is suggested that F.W.M.T. would have to undergo radical change in comparison to their R. and D.C. colleagues to learn and adopt financial control skills; to define the social work task; and to manage their staff.

In an attempt to integrate conceptually the elements of the decline process, Murray and Jick (1985) suggest a framework of four elements: problem definition process; substantive decisions; implementation process; and outcomes. The model is iterative as the authors are interested in the insights which accrue from linking rather than isolating these components. The significance of contextual and sub-cultural features in the decline process was addressed above and these components may with advantage be added to the Murray and Jick (1985) framework, thus increasing its utility.

Stringency Induced Innovation

The concept of organisational monetarism would be expected to predict that stringency would encourage positive innovation even if only in this context by accepting the job of managing expenditure reductions, and defining the social work task .

Managers did not regard resource reductions as stimulating innovation for, although changes were noted, members' involvement in reductions was generally regarded as having few of the positive outcomes predicted by organisational monetarism. Differences of opinion on the matter were more concerned with differing degrees of negative impact felt by members. Chapter VI contained details of conflictual changes at various levels in the organisation, noted particularly by F.W. managers. The way managers regarded the future is now considered.

Pessimistic Views of the Future

The future was not regarded with optimism for anticipated innovations were expressed in terms of halting or slowing down developments, either on a general, or on a specific level. Even the Director, who adopted a fairly complacent stance, said that

> things would get worse,

and his view was supported by middle managers. For example, one F.W. manager said reductions

> means a total block on new initiatives. It will be worse
> next year

and another said

> It's the beginning of the end for Social Services.

A less extreme, and generalised view was presented by another F.W. manager

> I don't see my role as justifying a cut in services and I see more conflictual relations with senior management especially with our team leader; we're not talking about dismantling of the service; it's a change in ethos.

F.W. managers believed their jobs were becoming less innovative and developmental and more maintenance orientated, with, as one of their number put it,

> a growing expenditure of energy on trying to cope with the effects of cuts.

R. and D.C.M.T. felt the same for as one said

> cuts have had little professional impact at the moment, but if there's another round, it's bound to affect and alter practice. We were beginning to pull together a professional strategy. Now professional growth has been stunted, it's been slowed down.

Even the member who was in favour of reductions mentioned their negative effect on the physical conditions in which he and his section worked;

> no heat in the building and stone floors,

and these would not be improved, he said, because of the reductions in expenditure. No one offered a positive view along the lines suggested by those theorists quoted in Chapter III who support organisational monetarism.

These theorists identified a causal connection between financial stringency and innovation, but were not concerned with managers' perceptions of such a connection. Absence of such perceptions on the part of managers in the organisation studied casts doubt on how far the concept of organisational monetarism is rooted in practice. This absence suggests that causation is more complex and less direct than predicted, and that intervening variables of sub-culture and context need to be taken into account in order to understand managerial responses to stringency.

Summary

Three assumptions of organisational monetarism were examined: a facility for financial management; quantifiability of task; and positive innovation induced by fewer resources. The behaviour of one organisation's middle management teams was compared. The sub-cultural feature of financial management experience, and the contextual features of pattern of spending, task arrangements, stage of professional development, and unionateness were considered. These features influenced the extent to which reductions management was acceptable at both a theoretical and practical level. The acceptance of the financial management task depended on the perceived familiarity and relevance it enjoyed in a group, whilst the feasibility of justifying and quantifying activities depended on the specificity of the activity. Less specific activities were more at risk from decision makers who were obliged to choose between the less and the more tangible. Pattern of spending, stage of professional development and degree of unionateness also influenced the ease or difficulty with which the reductions task could be managed.

Managers had negative perceptions of the innovations which resulted from reductions, and the assumptions inherent in the concept of organisational monetarism were therefore found to be open to question. The concepts of efficiency and cost effectiveness were not automatically accepted as relevant or even identified as an effect of financial stringency. This suggests that organisational monetarism does not provide an adequate means of understanding managerial responses to stringency. An alternative explanation, which focuses on the influence of features of sub-culture and context as they differentially affect management teams, provides a more useful means of analysing the variety of management responses.

9 The management of decline: a conclusion

Introduction

This concluding chapter reviews the contribution to knowledge, identifies areas for further research, and outlines the limitation of this work.

After setting out the major contributions of this research, and indicating its limitations, a model of managerial responses to expenditure is presented. This model provides a structure for the rest of the chapter as elements of it are elaborated by reference to organisational data. These are used to examine relevant theories critically and as a basis for indicating further research.

Explanations of managerial responses which focus on characteristics of reductions as a threat from the environment are examined and found to be inadequate. As an example, the concept of organisational monetarism, and the assumptions on which it is based, is elaborated. The task of recommending reductions is briefly described. Two sets of organisational factors, sub-cultures and contextual features, are then identified as they apply to specific management teams. The significance of these factors in providing managers with a means of managing the reductions task is then described. The degree of fit between organisational factors and the reductions task is explored in terms of the extent of threat to established practices and values the latter poses. The utility of rationality as an explanatory device is then examined.

The extent to which threat was routinised or resisted is apparent from the different responses that managers exhibited. These are described by reference to the two sets of organisational factors.

The results of managerial responses to stringency are then presented as costs and benefits to the organisation. In particular, cost, conflict, control, and innovation, are examined. Finally the management of diversity, a significant managerial task in times of stringency, is considered, using data from an intervention designed to resolve intergroup conflict.

The major contribution of this work is to the theory of managing expenditure reductions. Within this broad theme the influence of management sub-cultures is considered. Field data was obtained from three management teams in one Social Services Department: senior management (the Director's Management Team or D.M.T.) and middle management (Field Work Management Team or F.W.M.T. and Residential and Day Care Management Team or R. and D.C.M.T.).

It was discovered that whilst all managers perceived expenditure reductions as a threat, some routinised this threat by accepting and operationalising reductions (R. and D.C.M.T.), whilst others responded as to a crisis either by avoiding the issue (D.M.T.), or by voicing overt resistance (F.W.M.T.). The analysis focuses on why threat was interpreted as a crisis by some managers, but not by others, and thus on what determined different managerial responses.

Hermann (1963) identifies three factors which contribute to our perception of an event as a crisis: limited response time; the unexpected nature of the event; and the threat it presents to deeply held values, which Hermann terms priority values. Managers described the event of expenditure reductions as unexpected; all managers had a limited response time. Initially it appeared that different responses could therefore be analysed in terms of degree of perceived threat to priority values. This interpretation was popular amongst the organisation's managers, and coincided with the initial focus of the research on organisational sub-cultures.

It became apparent that whilst managerial values were an important factor in determining responses, they were an insufficient basis from which to analyse the empirical data. Additional organisational factors were also significant, because such factors were seen to inhibit or facilitate reductions management at an operational level. By identifying these significant factors, the research contributes to the theory of expenditure reductions management.

The analysis shows a causal relationship between internal factors of the organisational sub-units within which managers operate, and the degree to which reductions management is routinised or problematic. Sub-unit factors identified were management team sub-cultures and contextual features. As these factors differed for each management team, so the degree to which they were able to assimilate the phenomena of expenditure reductions varied. By exposing the variety of significant factors which influenced action, our understanding of the meaning managers attach to reductions, and their responses, is expanded. Effective reductions management can thus involve radical change, in respect of a number of factors in addition to the narrow focus on financial control found in some of the literature (Dworak: 1975; Green: 1974; Ogden: 1978; Pondy: 1964).

At the same time this work elaborates the diversity of managerial response to resource pressure, and the rationalities which underpin this. In particular, attention is drawn to the defensive strategies of avoidance, resistance and withdrawal. Diversity of response to stringency within organisations, and its implications, has not previously been explored to any great extent. In general, literature in this area has a macro-organisational focus. Theory derived from this level is tested and elaborated using data from the micro-level, the major focus of which is accounts by managers themselves. It became apparent that certain predicted responses such as a move towards strategic rationality, did not in fact occur, and that unpredicted ones such as withdrawal did.

The analysis is limited in that the research took place in the initial period when expenditure reductions became a management issue and was conducted over a period of months rather than years. Thus the significance of resource pressure long-term is not considered.

A focus on one organisation as a source of data raises the issue of whether the resultant analysis is generalisable. Whilst the data-base is limited, the analytical categories abstracted from it can be used in analyses of other organisations. Additionally the process of integrating theory based on the management of stringency elsewhere indicates that the experience of Social Service managers is by no means unique. Generalisations flow from elaborating analytical categories which are of general utility, and by establishing links at a theoretical level with other studies.

Below in Figure 4 is an explanatory model of the organisational factors which influenced managerial interpretations of, and responses to, the environmental threat presented by financial stringency. The resultant organisational costs and benefits are also indicated.

This model provides the structure for the remaining part of this chapter which examines each numbered box of the figure sequentially.

(1) Environmental Threat

The environmental threat of resource scarcity has been used to predict managerial responses. This perspective is based on the concept of organisational monetarism. Characteristics of the threat - source (political or rational, according to Levine (1978)), size, and speed - have also been utilised as a means of understanding managerial behaviour. These analyses and their usefulness are examined below.

Organisational Monetarism

The concept is made explicit using theories and prescriptions for managing organisations suffering financial stringency. An undefined version of organisational monetarism is found in much of the literature and figures more explicitly in political statements at ministerial level. The economic concept of monetarism emphasises the benefits of restricting the growth of the money supply (Donaldson: 1982; Harvey: 1983). Transposed to organisations, a positive and causal connection is predicted between reduced resources and innovation in the direction of efficiency and cost effectiveness.

A number of authors support the prediction that financial stringency results in organisational benefits. Such benefits include: the redeployment of resources (Biller: 1980), institutional reviews (Bogue: 1972), new and improved managerial practices (Cheit: 1971, 1973). Stringency can also

FIGURE 4
MANAGERIAL RESPONSES TO DECLINE

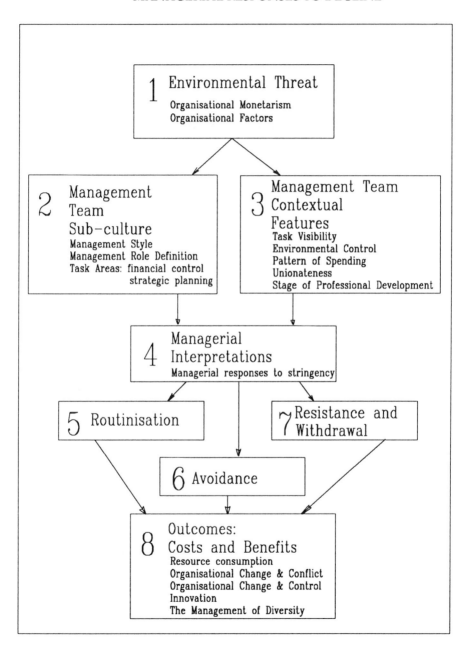

improve decision-making (March and Cohen: 1974); improve budgetary processes (Stewart: 1980); and lead to positive change and innovation (McTighe: 1979).

Five assumptions of organisational monetarism are identified and examined below: an orientation towards financial management; ease of task specification and measurement; rational decision-making (what Weber (1968) terms 'formal rationality'); positive innovation; and zero cost. The data does not support the over-riding importance of a tougher environment represented by resource scarcity as a determinant of managerial responses.

Other authors have focused on specific characteristics of financial stringency as an explanatory device. These are now considered.

Political and rational sources of decline are identified by Levine (1978) and Jick and Murray (1982) as a means of predicting whether managers will respond rationally or politically. Decline for all managers in the Social Services Department resulted from changing Government policy. The Local Authority responded by requiring reductions in departmental budgets. Though the political source of decline was the same, managers' responses were significantly varied as were the rationalities used to justify them. Thus the source of decline does not assist our analysis of the data.

Murray and Jick (1985), and Gill and Pratt (1986), refine the concept of organisational monetarism. They identify size and speed of reductions as significant in determining whether managers choose the efficiency or the effectiveness response (Whetton: 1981). The former involves doing less of the same; the latter, doing something different or innovating. Both sets of authors predict that only large speedy reductions will result in innovation, because only reductions of crisis proportions will stimulate change.

Yet crisis does not invariably result in innovation (Ford: 1981; Hermann: 1963; Staw et al; 1981). The data demonstrates that one management group which perceived the threat of reductions as a crisis was also the group which responded, not by innovating, but by voicing overt opposition, and then withdrawing from reduction-related activities. This study indicates no connection between perceived crisis and innovation.

Typologies of reduction characteristics are, though, potentially useful for research at the macro-level. In addition to the two categories used by Gill and Pratt (1986) - slow erosion and dramatic decrease - the research identifies a third one. The organisation experienced a sudden reduction in but this was not large, at three and a half per cent in absolute terms. It was a sudden, but incremental reduction.

Furthermore, a fourth category can be identified, where dramatic or large reductions take place over a number of years. Whether reductions exhibiting these characteristics occur and whether managers respond to them by innovation, increased efficiency or resistance would be an interesting area for further research.

The management task was to recommend reductions which had the least effect on clients, by examining all departmental spending areas and controlling spending in line with the allocated budget. There were to be no `sacred cows' and future service developments would depend on the re-allocation of existing funds rather than additional monies.

Organisational Factors

Two sets of organisational factors influenced the managers' interpretation of the expenditure reductions task: the sub-culture of their respective management teams, and features of the context within which each functioned. Whilst all managers regarded expenditure reductions as a threat, the extent to which threat was perceived as a crisis, or was routinised, depended on the fit between the sets of factors referred to above and the expenditure reductions task.

The impact of internal organisational factors on the implementation of reductions is noted by a minority of authors, such as Jick and Murray (1982), McTighe (1979), Rubin (1980), and Whetton (1981). As they worked at the macro-organisational level, they do not differentiate the influences such features have on organisational sub-units, in respect of degree or direction. This research examines both these areas at the micro-organisational level and, furthermore, identifies additional significant features. Finally, the framework for analysing decline management suggested by Murray and Jick (1985) is expanded by identifying an additional component, that of pre-existing organisational factors, as a pre-requisite for understanding managerial definitions of decline.

The two sets of organisational factors - managerial sub-cultures and contextual features - are now considered.

(2) Management Team Sub-Cultures

The analysis of culture in organisations is taken to a greater level of specificity than is usually found in the literature by discovering and examining the nature of management team sub-cultures, and in particular the influence these had on the implementation of expenditure reductions.

A view of cultural variety within organisations is in contradiction to the monolithic view of organisational cultures presented by Handy (1976), Jaques (1957), and Pettigrew (1979). Whilst there are references to sub-culture and group culture in, for example, Bennis (1969), and Silverzweig and Allen (1976), these remain unexamined except at the most general level. Similarly, what few references there are to culture in the literature on managing decline (Hirschhorn and Associates: 1983) focus on the organisation as a whole.

Sub-culture is defined as a group's typifications or 'taken for granted' ways of thinking and working which need to be known, but not invariably accepted, as a pre-requisite for acceptance as a competent member.

The hypothesis that management teams have their own individual sub-culture was supported. Five levels of specificity were used by members to identify group sub-cultures. Cultural maintenance was examined. The mechanics for suppressing intragroup differences were exposed, as were the means by which the group reinforced its view of itself and out-group members. This was done via the collective construction of routine and critical issues (Pettigrew: 1979); accounts of interactions with non-members; and by the process of collective behaviour exhibited at team meetings.

The dimensions of a group's sub-culture were used by its members to describe, explain and justify their actions both to each other and to outsiders, and to account for the actions of non-members. Sub-cultural norms provided a guide to action and attitudes, and a means of decision making.

This research thus contributes to our understanding of members' behaviour by examining how groups attach meaning to events, using collective typifications. The analysis is then taken to a more specific level by showing how cultures are identified and maintained.

Three aspects of a group sub-culture were identified as significant in influencing managers' responses to decline: the manner or style in which managers carry out their function, the definition of the manager's role, and the task areas.

Management Style

Field Work (F.W.) managers saw themselves for the most part as democratic, consultative and participative in their relations with fellow team members and with subordinates. Independence characterised their relations with senior management. Residential and Day Care (R. and D.C.) managers were perceived as directing in their relations with staff, and as accepting direction from above. They saw themselves as both giving and accepting direction. Action was more important than consultation, whereas Field Work managers were perceived as more consultative and theoretical, rather than practical. The D.M.T. was seen as being controlled by their leader and indecisive with a focus on short-term rather than strategic issues. They followed directions from above, and directed those below.

Management Role Definition

In discussing and evaluating behaviour, seven concepts were used: realism, responsibility (both to a significant reference group, and for a task); values, maturity, caring, emotionalism and participation. Significantly different interpretations of the manager's role were identified. These were evaluated in terms of perceived `correct' and `incorrect' managerial behaviour, rather than as examples of plurality, or different but equally valid action.

Different interpretations of the manager's role revolved around who defined reality, managers' values and tasks, and the limits of participation in decision making. Senior management defined these matters for R. and D.C.M.T., whereas in F.W.M.T. other groups and individuals were regarded as legitimate influences. As a consequence and because they provided definitions which conflicted with those of senior management, F.W. managers were less certain of their role than their R. and D.C. colleagues.

Task Area: financial control

The organisation's two middle management teams differed in their experience of and interest in financial management in general, and control in particular. In R. and D.C.M.T. financial control was a taken for granted aspect of the group's culture, of which they had experience and skills. F.W.M.T. in contrast were uninterested in, and unfamiliar with, financial control. This resulted from their history of resource abundance, supported by Council policy, and a perceived distinction and contradiction between financially and professionally based decisions. Unlike their R. and D.C. colleagues, they had no responsibility for financial control. Thus whilst one group had the financial management competence assumed by organisational monetarism, the other did not. Thereby, this assumption could not be generalised. The data supports those authors (Cazalis: 1979; Cheit: 1973: Cyert: 1975) who identify lack of familiarity with, and interest in, financial control as a problem for those managing decline.

In addition, the analysis differentiates the extent to which this is the case by demonstrating that absence of financial control is not an issue for all managers in organisations faced with decline.

Only Cyert (1975) suggests how this problem may be overcome: through participation which leads to the incorporation of productivity goals. The pre-supposition of willingness to participate was not apparent in the data; the group which lacked financial skills and interest also resisted, and then withdrew from the task of reductions.

Further research could usefully discover what, if any, steps are taken to change managers' attitudes to financial management and/or to provide them with financial management skills. It is also of interest to speculate on the relation between the two: that is, the extent to which the acquisition of skills changes attitudes or attitudes inhibit the acquisition of new skills. Similarly, one could question how far managers learn by experience of the need for financial control when left without money part way through the financial year: or alternatively, whether financial managers or administrators who already have the positive attitudes and skills, take over the management role, as Cheit (1971, 1973) reports. The significance of a professional perspective to the management of stringency is considered below, under `Stage of Professional Development'.

Task Area: strategic planning

Strategic planning was not a significant task for either D.M.T. or F.W.M.T.. As we have seen the D.M.T. focused on short-term, not strategic issues. A lack of strategic planning was demonstrated by the definition of the reductions task. No priorities were indicated, and managers were invited to recommend reductions in other departments as well as their own. Similarly

F.W.M.T. had devised no formal priorities; in fact their aim was to provide a universal service. Managerial groups then do not invariably value or formulate strategic plans and an unplanned approach influences responses to expenditure reductions.

Further research could usefully discover the stage at which the significance of strategic planning is accepted and operationalised. Additionally it would be interesting to learn how this is achieved. Alternatively it would be useful to discover if managers can deal with expenditure reductions in the longer term, without devising some form of strategy to guide their actions.

(3) Management Team Contextual Features

The two middle-management teams operated within different organisational contexts. Features associated with these facilitated or inhibited reductions management. These contextual features were: task visibility, environmental control, pattern of spending, unionateness and stage of professional development.

Task Visibility

The ability to specify tasks and outcomes is of benefit in circumstances of reduced resources. Divisions' respective task technologies determined the degree of task specificity.

F.W. provided a community-based, generic and universal service. R. and D.C. was establishment-based and provided physical care services to specific and restricted client groups. R. and D.C. managers could specify tasks and outcomes by reference to clients in care and to the establishments in which this care took place. As F.W. activities took place in the community there was little tangible evidence of their work.

Clarity and visibility of task was significant, in three respects. Firstly, less easily defined tasks were less well protected from those who had to make difficult choices about reductions. Conversely, specifiable tasks aided decision-making on priorities. Thirdly, specifiable tasks were more easily quantified and fitted into a budgetary-based information system. This final point on quantification relates directly to the assumption found in organisational monetarism that task measurement is unproblematic.

This, though, is not invariably the case, as this research demonstrates. Not all tasks are easily quantifiable, (for example, Balderstone (1972), Bozeman and Slusher (1979), Cyert (1975), Starbuck et al (1978)). The argument is perhaps best summarised by Pfeffer and Salancik (1978):

> That which is measured is attended to and that which is not is ignored. It is not surprising that the first reaction to organisational problems typically involves solutions focusing on efficiency dimensions for frequently that is the only thing the organisation can measure (p. 81).

An area of further research concerns the extent to which tasks that cannot be easily defined are included in a budgetary decision-making process and whether the provision of professional information noted in the data becomes routinised, thereby changing the information base of the budgetary processes.

Managers of qualitative tasks may attempt to educate decision makers about these tasks, to insure themselves against being an easy target for reductions. Alternatively managers may in some way make their tasks more tangible, again as a protective device against cut-backs.

Environmental Control

Given the task technology of each division, the degree to which the client environment could be controlled differed significantly. Establishments provided a built-in control mechanism, based on physical limits of buildings. No such control was available for community-based services.

Further research could usefully discover whether over time, more control of community-based clients is formally exerted by restricting the definition of 'the client' and/or by prioritising the needs of client groups.

Pattern of Spending

Pattern of spending focuses on the degree of variety of spending areas available to managers making reductions. In the F.W. division spending was primarily on salaries for professional staff. R. and D.C.M.T. controlled a primarily on salaries for professional staff. R. and D.C.M.T. controlled a greater variety of spending areas, including the upkeep of establishments. Reducing staff, the principal option open to F.W. managers, was seen as a much more difficult management task than reducing building maintenance.

Unionateness

The F.W. division was strongly unionised at both staff and management level, whereas R. and D.C. was not. The union (N.A.L.G.O.) adopted a strategy of opposition to reductions, including non-participation in reduction related issues.

This strategy was thus a significant factor in determining the parameters of managerial behaviour for one group of managers but not for the other.

The research elaborates the dimension of unionateness identified by McTighe (1979) as a factor which influences implementation of reductions, by showing that the significance of this influence varies within an organisation. Further research could usefully discover how long managers and staff continue to support their union's policy, and indeed whether and how this policy is subject to revision.

Stage of Professional Development

Prior to financial stringency becoming an issue, the F.W. and R. and D.C. divisions were at different stages of development in respect of service provision. F.W. managers had developed a professional awareness of what should be provided and this was reflected in current practice. R. and D.C. were just beginning to develop; their professional awareness and practice were rudimentary. The meaning of reductions, in terms of professional knowledge and practice, had greater significance for managers of developed service. Reconciling this with service reductions was thus a difficult issue for one group, but less difficult for another.

Further research would be useful to discover whether the dimension of greater professional awareness is invariably an inhibiting influence in cutbacks, and how this issue is managed. It would also be useful to learn if the inverse relationship between professional awareness and financial control skills found in this organisation is apparent elsewhere.

This work aids our understanding of managerial responses to expenditure reductions by locating these within a framework provided by two sets of organisational factors: group sub-cultures and contextual features. Group sub-cultures determine the extent to which managers value or have experience of strategic planning and financial control. Contextual features determine the degree to which expenditure reductions can be operationalised. Inhibiting and facilitating features within the internal environment of each management group are most significant in influencing responses to financial stringency. Stringency alone does not promote the automatic and uniform response predicted by organisational monetarism.

Further research is indicated to discover the variety of additional influencing factors within and between organisations, the degree of their significance to managers, and the extent to which their influence is recognised or ignored.

(4) Managerial Interpretations

The focus on sub-cultures and contextual features demonstrates the degree and complexity of change required of different management groups if the threat of reductions is to be managed rather than avoided or resisted. It is this degree of change which determined the managers' interpretation of the threat, and resulted in the responses described in the next section. Here the degree of change required for the reductions task to be operationalised is examined together with the utility of `rationality' as a device to predict and explain managerial responses.

For the R. and D.C.M.T., no change was necessary to the group sub-culture or contextual features for the threat of reductions to be accommodated. It was therefore interpreted in a routine manner, and was not regarded as problematic.

For F.W. managers, on the other hand, the threat was not susceptible to routinisation without a radical change in their sub-culture, such as accepting the value of financial control. Similarly all the contextual features of their internal environment also required change for reductions to be managed. The type of change required included controlling their client environments, and making their community-based task more visible. These managers interpreted reductions as a crisis, and responded firstly by attempting to remove the threat, and then by ignoring it.

The D.M.T. fell somewhere between the two extremes presented above. The group valued bureaucratic responses, and thus accepted the reductions task as a routine issue, but they did not value strategic planning. To alter both values and practices in this task area involved radical change and was interpreted as a threat. They avoided the threat, in the short term, by delegating the decision-making tasks.

Thus managers generally did not interpret the threat of reductions as necessitating change to their traditional values and practices, nor to the contexts within which they worked. In fact the degree of change required to sub-culture and context determined whether reductions were interpreted as a routine issue, a threat, or a crisis.

The research demonstrates that assumptions of 'rationality', either formal or strategic, which are associated with the concept of organisational monetarism, are misguided and unhelpful in analysing managerial responses. Glennester's (1980) hypothesis of multiple rationalities was confirmed and extended. Each management team responded using a variety of rationalities, or logics for action, which strongly reflected the influence of their respective sub-culture and the contexts within which they operated.

Thus D.M.T. operated in terms of bureaucratic and administrative rationality, but not strategic rationality. R. and D.C.M.T. operated on the basis of bureaucratic, professional and political rationalities. F.W.M.T. rejected strategic, bureaucratic and administrative rationalities preferring professional, task definition, ideological, industrial relations, and political rationalities.

Glennester's (1980) hypothesis was elaborated as follows: additional rationalities to those he identified were apparent; bureaucratic and administrative forms of rationality were isolated from professional rationality (whereas Glennester dealt with the three together); a particular rationality was not confined to a specific group: groups behaved in terms of a number of rationalities; and there were competing rationalities within as well as between groups. The assumption that strategic, or formal rationality predominates in reductions was not supported.

Before examining managerial responses, the significance of size of reduction to managerial interpretation is considered. Briefly, F.W.M.T. anticipated losing, and in fact did lose, more money than their R. and D.C.

colleagues. In comparison with the organisational factors outlined above, relative scale of reductions was not of overriding significance. F.W. managers responded to the threat of reductions as such, rather than to reductions of a particular size. R. and D.C. managers maintained a stance of following orders throughout,and for D.M.T. differential size of reduction was not an issue.

Greater reductions though, added to the sense of threat and made the management task more difficult; lesser reductions had the reverse effect. But size of reductions alone does not assist our understanding of why these three management groups interpreted reductions in the ways they did.

Managerial Responses to Stringency

The research identifies the diversity of managerial responses to be found in one organisation. It recognises, and assists our understanding of, defensive tactics which are infrequently considered in the literature.

With few exceptions, theory in the field assumes co-operation from managers, and a homogeneous response from organisations. Resistance is seldom considered; it is usually contrasted with co-operation and defined as either short-term (Hills and Mahoney: 1978; Levine: 1978), or predictable (Behn: 1976; Biller: 1976; Levine: 1978), and based only on self-interest (Biller: 1980; Caiden: 1980; Greenhalgh and McKersie: 1980). None of these analyses was confirmed by the data. Resistance was not a tactic considered by R. and D.C.M.T. On the other hand, F.W. managers did not co-operate for at least twelve months. They justified their actions by reference to client and staff interests, that is, by factors in addition to self-interest. Similarly, withdrawal as a managerial tactic has received little attention. It has usually been defined as leaving the organisation (Levine: 1979; Scott: 1976) or absence due to industrial action (Hirschman: 1970).

Analysis of the empirical data resulted in a typology of responses which extends our understanding of resistance and withdrawal. In addition to co-operation, or routinisation, there were two defensive responses: avoidance and resistance/ withdrawal. These responses are now considered in the context of the organisational factors already outlined. (See Figure 4, above.)

(5) Routinisation

R. and D.C. managers were able to routinise the reductions task, and thus co-operate, because their team's sub-culture provided support. Collectively, managers valued direction and taking action with minimum consultation; senior management defined their role. The group valued and had experience of financial control.

The contextual features of their internal environment facilitated rather than inhibited reductions management: task visibility and environmental control were high, they had a varied pattern of spending, with low unionateness and professional awareness.

(6) Avoidance

Bion's (1961) defensive reactions were used to produce a typology which focuses on the degree of flight or fight apparent, and the extent to which reductions tasks were rejected or accepted.

Avoidance is defined as denying those aspects of the threat which necessitate change in a team's sub-culture (such as strategy formulation) but accommodates those aspects which do not (such as following orders). The D.M.T. avoided formulating a strategy for reductions by delegating the task to middle managers, and by denying their own responsibility. But by following orders from councillors they did not avoid the issue of expenditure reductions completely.

Though this team operated within the context provided by both middle management teams, their response was in terms of R. and D.C.M.T. only, that is, they assumed that the organisational factors which applied to R. and D.C.M.T. applied equally to their F.W. colleagues. This however was not the case.

(7) Resistance and Withdrawal

Resistance is defined as overt opposition to remove the threat. Withdrawal is defined as refusal to participate in any reductions-related task, but otherwise to continue managing as in the past.

F.W.M.T.'s sub-culture provided little or no support for routinising reductions management. Strategic planning and financial control were devalued and did not form part of the group's experience. The sole right of senior management to define their role was denied. They rejected direction and valued collective decision-making and consultation.

The context within which they worked inhibited routinisation: task visibility and environmental control were low; spending was restricted primarily to staff; and unionateness and professional awareness were high.

This group exhibited both resistance and withdrawal responses, in the following sequence.

After initially participating to some extent in recommending reductions, due to 'shock' (Fink et al: 1971), F.W. managers resisted by voicing opposition both internally, and to councillors. They temporarily withdrew their services. When reductions were decided, and were less than anticipated, the threat receded. Internal debate on the rights and wrongs of this strategy disrupted the initial cohesion to pursue overt opposition, and F.W. managers' confined their response to one of withdrawal.

Further research could usefully discover whether resistance and withdrawal responses are always sequential, as above, or whether they are cyclical. Additionally, research is indicated in respect of the development of managerial responses longitudinally, to learn how long managers can continue to adopt the defensive strategies outlined above. At the same time, it would be of interest to know what, if any, attempts are made by superiors to change these strategies.

(8) Outcomes: Costs and Benefits

The analysis shows that managing and resisting reductions involved a high cost both in terms of human resources, and in human relations within the organisation. The zero-cost assumption of organisational monetarism was not supported. Increased conflict and control were noted though not, as they are frequently presented, as organisational-wide phenomena. The analysis locates costs and benefits within specific inter and intra group interactions. Finally the presence or absence of innovation is considered.

Resource Consumption

A number of writers who otherwise support the concept of organisational monetarism refer to the high cost of reductions. These include, Balderstone (1972), Hirschhorn (1983b) and David (1979). The data indicates that decline management is not cost free, even for managers who routinise the task. For example both F.W.M.T. and D.M.T. spent time discussing the areas of conflict within their teams noted below. Similarly, F.W.M.T. and R. and D.C.M.T. spent time discussing and disputing the 'correct' way to manage reductions.

It would be a useful area of further research to compute the direct financial costs of managing reductions. It would also be instructive to discover the opportunity costs of diverting resources from other activities to managing stringency.

Organisational Change and Conflict

Theory acknowledges an increase in conflict in stringency, but in fairly general terms. This research contributes to our understanding of stringency-provoked conflict by contrasting the extent of conflict within and between particular management groups. In addition to the sources of conflict identified as resources in the literature (Scott: 1974; Levine: 1978, 1979), or the goals for which resources are used (Cyert and March: 1963; Gill: 1981), the research introduces managerial responses to decline management. As well as causing conflict, decline management also promoted harmony.

With stringency, F.W. managers reported more conflict within their management team, and in their relations with R. and D.C.M.T. and D.M.T.. Members of both these latter groups confirmed this. Within D.M.T. there were strong differences of opinion too, but there was no conflict either within R. and D.C.M.T. or between this team and its senior managers. Thus increased conflict is not an inevitable result of financial stringency, nor does conflict occur within and between all management teams.

In F.W.M.T. competition for resources resulted in conflict because such competition was unacceptable in their team sub-culture. Different views of the best way to manage reductions produced conflict in F.W.M.T. and D.M.T. because the sub-cultural norms of each group were challenged by the new tasks of reductions management. In F.W.M.T. the debate concerned whether to resist, withdraw or co-operate. In the D.M.T. the debate concerned whether to devise strategic plans. Lack of co-operation on the part of F.W.M.T. was a source of conflict between that group and both R. and D.C. and D.M.T. Conversely agreement on the 'right' way to manage reductions was a source of harmony between the last two groups, because they shared what Sherif's (1953) term a superordinate goal: the management of reductions in terms of the presented task.

This work identifies a new source of conflict: how best to respond to the change associated with reductions. At a deeper level of analysis, conflict is explained by reference to definitions of 'correct' responses provided by a team's sub-culture.

Organisational Change and Control

Cazalis (1979) and Cyert (1978) recommend increased control as a means of managing reductions. Similarly Levine et al (1981) and Rubin (1980) discovered that centralised control facilitates decline management. Only F.W. managers perceived an increase in control by senior managers, which is consistent with a group which values its independence from such control. Yet F.W. managers withdrew, thereby abdicating control. This apparent contradiction is partially resolved by the fact that the group did not want control of decision making on service priorities, nor control of spending. Whilst R. and D.C. managers did not note an increase in control, senior management delegated control of service prioritisation.

Increased control in times of stringency is qualified in two ways. Firstly by reference to release of control by withdrawal or delegation: managers may accept or reject control rather than have it taken from them. Secondly the research identifies a task area over which no one wanted control: service prioritisation. It seems that centralised control is not an all-embracing phenomenon but varies with the circumstances of the particular case.

Innovation

The data shows that reductions did not lead to inventiveness and innovation. Rather there was a change towards a more conflict-ridden culture, which was noted earlier.

Changes in managerial practice were not implemented either by F.W.M.T. or D.M.T. No change was reported either in R. and D.C.M.T. The future was regarded with apprehension. Reductions were seen to inhibit professional developments, to increase conflict, and to demand a greater expenditure of energy on debating and on coping with the effects of a smaller budget.

The assumption of positive outcomes was found to be incorrect. In fact the reverse occurred and reductions produced changes which in general did not facilitate task performance.

The Management of Diversity

This research exposes the diversity of managerial interpretations and responses that can be expected in times of expenditure reductions, and explains this diversity in terms of the fit between features of sub-culture and context on the one hand, and the task of reductions management on the other. Any effective prescription for decline management must therefore take account of the cultural and contextual diversity within an organisation.

Diversity needs to be managed rather than avoided if full use of resources is to be effected. A means of doing so might be to examine the basis for different responses, as outlined above. By becoming aware of what facilitates and inhibits reduction management, possible changes may be identified and action taken.

In this case senior management did not manage diversity. Instead they supported a unitary approach to the management task exemplified by the behaviour of R. and D.C.M.T. Additionally they used a value-based, and therefore partial, explanation of unacceptable behaviour on the part of managers. The analysis of the intervention in Chapter 7 underlines the significance of the unitary perspective, and the threat which an alternative perspective based on diversity posed.

The analysis of managerial responses to decline in the short term highlights a number of policy issues for the management of expenditure reductions in the longer term. The most significant of these is whether or not an organisational strategy has been reformulated in the light of financial stringency. In the absence of such a reformulation it is predicted that the managerial responses and organisational costs identified in this study will continue, to the detriment of service provision. Control and conflict will increase, as will the resources needed to be devoted to managing these matters; there will be little creativity and innovation. Managers will either continue to 'follow orders', that is, collaborate or pretend to do so, in an ad hoc manner, with no reference to strategic considerations in respect of service provision and without the benefit of guidance provided by a planed strategy. Alternatively, they will continue to withdraw symbolically from activities associated with stringency as a means of demonstrating support for an anti-cuts stance and the organisation's pre-reductions strategy. Of course nether of these responses are organisationally desirable and they are to be avoided particularly for the long term. Managers need firstly to reassess the objectives of the organisation and then develop a strategy to achieve them.

Within this strategy they will then need to choose one or more of three funding options.

Firstly, generate income from new sources in order to maintain current levels of service and/or to finance new service developments. Secondly, reduce services to reflect the reduction in resources and finally, provide the same services despite the lower level of funding, that is, provide services more economically.

Choices such as these are only meaningful within an overall organisational service-provision strategy and the absence of such strategic thinking will inhibit effective reductions management. The work demonstrates that assertions such as Scott's (1976).

> Can managers manage decline? Of course they can. The issue is not being unable to deal with decline, but wanting to deal with it (p. 56).

are mistaken. Managing decline involves both wanting to and being able to.

Appendices

Appendix I
Management Team Perceptions

The information set out below was obtained at an early stage in the action intervention. Both middle-management teams (F.W. and R and D.C.) were separately asked to generate descriptive terms in respect of:

    (a) their self-image;
    (b) their image of the other management team;
    (c) the other management team's view of them.

This data formed the basis for the exchange of inter-group perceptions referred to in Chapter 7.

Field Work Management Team

Self Image	Image of R. and D.C.	R. and D.C.'s image of F.W.
purposeless	hierarchical	unionised
non-authoritarian	authoritarian	pretentious
consultative	old fashioned	holier than thou
participative	inefficient	articulate
confronting	defensive	overbearing

Self Image	Image of R. and D.C.	R. and D.C.'s image of F.W.
unrealistic	fraught	anarchic
incohesive	radical	defensive
committed	conservative,	impractical
undisciplined	inflexible	arrogant
pessimistic	undermanned	selfish
frustrated	caring	sophisticated
daunted	hard-working	envious of them
nostalgic	purposeful	faltering
attractive	over-ambitious	mischievous
facetious	friendly	unco-operative
tolerant	organisationally remote	elitist
interesting	boring	intolerant
talented	gaining confidence	high powered
competitive	over controlled	challenging
vulnerable	limited	unrealistic
defensive	inefficient	well-meaning
self-deprecating		smarter
enthusiastic		introspective
hard-working		indecisive
supportive		verbose
unsure		political
accessible		intelligent
unsupported		intellectually-capable

Residential and Day Care Management Team

Self Image	Image of F.W.	F.W.'s image of R. and D.C.
Nuts & bolts: corporate	naive	authoritarian
Generalities: semi-corporate	political	acquiescent
Professional: corporate	inconclusive	non-corporate
	long-winded	fragmented
	corporate	non-general non-inexperience of
	inexperience of residential situation	F.W. situations
positive	perceived superiority	over-centralised
self-critical	non-understanding	insular
caring	unrealistic	motivated
internal isolation	powerful	a-political
progressive	threatened	inferiority complex
honest	professional	demanding
efficient	homogeneous	higher expectations
need to develop group support	divided	favoured
	presumptuous	efficient
	vociferous	uncommunicative
	negative synergy	
	collective	

Appendix II
Summary of the Report
to the
Social Services Department

1.   Introduction

The report provides data feedback, analysis and recommendations on the effects of expenditure reductions.   It focuses on the Department's three management teams and their interactions. Three sources of data were used: interviews, observation and documents.

2.   Background

Traditionally F.W. occupied a superior position within the Department, though this is being challenged by recent developments in R. and D.C.. The D.D. is also A.D. for R. and D.C.. A new A.D.F.W. was recruited at the time the requirement for reductions was introduced.   Recommendations on reductions were invited by senior management (S.M.) from middle management. F.W. lost more resources than R. and D.C. as the protection of the latter division was a priority.

3. Definitions of the Cuts

Various terms used to describe the cuts and their effects are identified; for example, zero growth and negative growth. Operationally the term 'the cuts' was used to refer to the relevant budgetary processes and to managing the effects of reductions, together with the imposition or increase of charges. The majority of members regarded the effects of the cuts as being negative.

4. Responses

S.M. referred the matter of recommendations to middle managers with little guidance. Subsequently S.M. made recommendations to councillors. R. and D.C.M.T. managed the cuts and came up with recommendations for the required amount. F.W.M.T. resisted the cuts. On the first occasion they made recommendations below the required amount, on the second they suggested an across the board percentage cut. Services in this division were withdrawn on two occasions. Each service division recommended cuts in the other. Both provided councillors with information on the effects of the cuts.

5. Reasons

S.M. saw prioritisation as a job for councillors. Like R. and D.C. they saw participation as a manager's responsibility and as a way to influence outcomes. F.M. resisted managing, again as an influencing strategy, and because of the perceived negative effects of reductions. These were at variance with their professional and personal values. They stated they could not manage, in the absence of guidance from above and in view of the conflicting messages from staff and S.M.

6.   Interpretations

For the resisting group, managing was seen variously as supporting government policy, as a typical response from an over-controlled group, and as masking the effects of the cuts. They saw S.M. pushing difficult decisions down to an inappropriately low level within the organisation, rather than accepting these as their own responsibility. The differential nature of the cuts was seen as indicating a dislike of F.W.'s area of work, a settling of old scores and as a punishment for resisting the cuts. For those who managed, resistance was seen as unprofessional, irresponsible, and the result of being influenced by personal and political rather than workplace values. By and large, differences were interpreted in terms of differing philosophies and styles of management.

7.   Effects

For F.W. the effects on the service, staff and intragroup relations were seen to be extremely disruptive. The effects on intergroup relations, that is, between R. and D.C.M.T. and F.W.M.T., and between the latter and D.M.T., were negatively perceived. Responses to the cuts became a way of judging organisational members.

8.   Action

The aim of this action was to improve relations between R. and D.C.M.T. and F.W.M.T. by giving them the opportunity to share their perceptions of each other, specify problems and seek solutions. Perceptions were generated and shared at an initial meeting. Problems raised were, for example, the roles of the representative and the bridge builder, the united front presented by F.W.M.T. in intergroup discussion, and different responses to cuts management.

9.   Situational Variables

A number of variables are identified which make it difficult to manage cuts. These fall into two categories: task and finance. In the former area, the social work task, environmental control, unionisation, stages of development, task specificity, justifiability, and quantification, are considered; in the latter area, financial skills, spending areas, joint responsibility and the differential size of reductions, are covered. A comparison is made between F.W.M.T. to have a more difficult position to manage over and above particular management styles and philosophies.

10.   Recommendations

F.W.M.T. and D.M.T. should negotiate their respective role requirements in the areas of prioritisation and managing the cuts, that is F.W. should agree to manage the effects in return for S.M. agreeing to prioritise the cuts. In addition, discussions should take place on the most effective way of exerting influence, based on the strategy of supplying information. This, it is suggested, can only be done in the context of a dialogue between union members and S.M. to clarify the roles of staff and management in relation to managing the effects of the cuts.

Bibliography

Balderston, F.E., *Varieties of Financial Crisis*, Berkeley, California, Ford Foundation (1972)

Bebbington, A. & Ferlie, E., *Budgeting and Planning in the Social Services Department in the Face of Cutbacks*, Canterbury, Personal Social Services Research Unit, University of Kent, Discussion paper No.172, September 1980

Beck, B., `Cooking welfare studies' in Habenstein, R.W. (Ed), *Pathways to Data*, Chicago, Aldine (1970), pp 7-29

Becker, H., *Sociological Work*, London, Allen Lane (1971)

Beckhard, R., *Organisational Development: Strategies and Models*, Reading, Massachusetts, Addison-Wesley (1969)

Behn, R.D., `Closing the Massachusetts public training schools', *Policy Science,* Vol.7, No.2, June 1976, pp 151-171

Behn, R.D., `Leadership for cut-back management: the use of corporate strategy', *Public Administration Review*, Vol.40, No.6, Nov/Dec. 1980, pp 613-620

Bennis, W.G., *Organisational Development: its Nature, Origins and Prospects,* Reading, Massachusetts, Addison-Wesley (1969)

Berger, M.B., `Two paradoxes in managing decline' in CHUNG, K.H. (Ed), *Proceedings of the Annual Meeting of The Academy of Management,* New York, Academy of Management (1982), pp 334-338

Biller, R.P., `On tolerating policy and organisational termination: some design considerations', *Policy Science,* Vol.7, No.2, June 1976, pp 133-149

Biller, R.P., `Leadership tactics in retrenchment', *Public Administration Review,* Vol.40, No.6, Nov/Dec 1980, pp 604-609

Billings, R.S., Milburn, T.W. & Schaalman, M.L., `A model of crisis perception: a theoretical and empirical analysis', *Administrative Science Quarterly,* Vol.25, No.2, June 1980, pp 300-316

Bion, W.R., *Experience in Groups,* London, Tavistock (1961)

Blake, R.R., Shepard, H.A. & Mouton, J.S., *Managing Intergroup Conflict in Industry,* Huston, Texas, Gulf (1964)

Blumer, H., `Society as symbolic interaction' in Rose, A.N. (Ed), *Human Behaviour and Social Processes,* London, Routledge and Regan Paul (1971), pp 179-192

Bouge, E.G., `Alternatives to the growth - progress syndrome', *Education Forum,* Vol.37, No.1, Nov. 1972, pp 35-43

222

Boulding, K.E., `The management of decline', *Change*, Vol.7, No.5, June 1975, pp 8-9 & 64

Bozeman, B. & Slusher, E.A., `Scarcity and environmental stress in public organisations', *Administration and Society*, Vol.11, No.3, Nov. 1979, pp 335-355

Brown, L.D., `"Research Action": organisational feedback, understanding and change', *Journal of Applied Behavioural Science*, Vol.8, No.6, Nov/Dec. 1972, pp 697-711

Burns, T. & Stalker, G.M., *The Management of Innovation*, London, Tavistock (1966)

Caiden, N., `Negative financial management: a backward look at fiscal stress' in Levine, C.H. & Rubin, I. (Eds) *Fiscal Stress and Public Policy*, Beverly Hills, Sage (1980), pp 135-157

Carnegie Foundation for the Advancement of Teaching, *More Than Survival*, San Fransisco, Jossey-Bass (1975)

Cazalis, P., `The University of the '80s: managing austerity', *International Journal of Institutional Management in Higher Education*, Vol.3, No.1, May 1979, pp 33-47

Cheit, E.F., *The New Depression in Higher Education*, New York, McGraw-Hill (1971)

Cheit, E.F., *The New Depression in Higher Education - two years later*, Berkeley, California, The Carnegie Commission on Higher Education (1973)

Cicourel, A.L., *Method and Measurement in Sociology*, New York, Free Press (1964)

Clark, A.W., `Sanction: a critical element in action research', *Journal of Applied Behavioural Studies*, Vol.8, No.6, Nov/Dec. 1972, pp 713-731

Clark, M., `On the concept of sub-culture', *British Journal of Sociology*, Vol.25, No.4, Dec. 1974, pp 428-441

Cohen, H., *The Demonics of Bureaucracy: problems of change in a government agency*, Ames, Iowa, Iowa State University Press, 1965

Coser, L., *The Function of Social Conflict*, London, Routledge & Kegan Paul (1956)

Cressey, R.R., `Prison Organisations' in March, J.G. (Ed), *Handbook of Organisations*, Chicago, Rand McNally (1965), pp 1023-1070

Cyert, R.M., `Management of non-profit organisations, with emphasis on universities' in Cyert, R.M. (Ed), *The Management of Non-Profit Organisations*, Lexington, Massachusetts, Lexington Books (1975), pp 7-32

Cyert, R.M., `The management of universities of constant or declining size', *Public Administration Review*, Vol.38, No.4, July/August 1978, pp 344-349

Cyert. R.M. & March, J.S., *A Behavioural Theory of the Firm*, Englewood Cliffs, New Jersey, Prentice Hall (1963)

Dalton, M., *Men Who Manage*, New York, John Wiley & Sons (1959)

David, E., `Benefit-cost analysis in state and local investment decisions', *Public Administration Review*, Vol.39, No.1, Jan/Feb 1979, pp 23-26

Davies, J.L. & Morgan, A.W., *The politics of institutional change under conditions of instability and contraction*, (Paper delivered to Leverhume Seminar on Institutional Adaption and Change), Bristol Polytechnic, September 1981

Delaney, W., `Some field notes on the problems of access in organisational research', *Administrative Science Quarterly*, Vol.5, No.3, September 1960, pp 448-457

Delaney, W., `The development and decline of patrimonial and bureaucratic administrations', *Administrative Science Quarterly*, Vol.7, No.4, December 1963, pp 458-501

Donaldson, P., *10x Economics*, Harmondsworth, Penguin (1982)

Duncan, R.B., `Characteristics of organisational environment and perceived uncertainty', *Administrative Science Quarterly*, Vol.17, No.3, September 1972, pp 313-327

Dworak, R.J., `Economising in public organisations', *Public Administration Review*, Vol.35, No.2, March/April 1975, pp 158-165

Eldridge, J.E.T., *Industrial Disputes: essays in the sociology of industrial relations*, London, Routledge and Kegan Paul (1968)

Fabozzi, F.J., `Financial aspects in managing non-profit organisations' in CYERT, R.M. (Ed), *The Management of Non-Profit Organisations*, Lexington, Massachusetts, Lexington Books (1975), pp 73-78

Ferlie, E., *Directory of Initiatives in Community Care for the Elderly*, Canterbury, Personal Social Services Research Unit, University of Kent, Discussion paper 148, Feb. 1980

Ferie, E. & Judge, K., *Retrenchment and Rationality in the Personal Social Services*, Canterbury, Personal Social Services Research Unit, University of Kent, Discussion paper No.173, October 1980

Fink, S.L., Beak, J. & Taddeo, K., `Organisational crisis and change', *Journal of Applied Behavioural Sciences*, Vol.7, No.1, Jan/Feb. 1971, pp 15-41

Flanders, A., *Fawley Productivity Agreement*, London, Faber (1964)

Ford, J.D., `The occurrence of structural hysteresis in declining organisations', *The Academy of Management Review*, Vol.5, No.4, October 1980, pp 589-598

225

Ford, J.D., `The management of organisational crisis', *Business Horizons*, Vol.24, No.3, May/June 1981, pp 10-16

Fordyce, J.K. & Wiel, R., *Managing With People*, Reading, Massachusetts, Addison-Wesley (1971)

Foster, M., `An introduction to the theory and practice of action research in work organisations', *Human Relations*, Vol.25, No.6, December 1972, pp 529-556

Fowler, A., `Local government manpower and the cuts', *Personnel Management*, Vol.12, No.9, Sept. 1980, pp 32-36

Fox, A., `Industrial sociology and industrial relations' in Flanders, A. (Ed), *Collective Bargaining: selective readings*, Harmondsworth, Penguin (1969), pp 360-409

Frame, P.G., *Managing Research: scientist meets bureaucrat*, Unpublished M.Sc.thesis, Department of Management Studies, Sheffield City Polytechnic, 1979

Frances, R.G. & Stone, R.C., *Service and Procedure in Bureaucracy*, Minneapolis, University of Minnesota (1956)

Freeman, J. & Hannan, M.T., `Growth and decline processes in organisations', *American Sociological Review*, Vol.40, No.2, April 1975, pp 215-228

Garfinkel, H., `The rational properties of scientific and commonsense activities' in Giddens, A. (Ed), *Positivism and Sociology*, London, Heinemann (1975), pp 53-73

Geer. B., `Studying a college' in Habenstein, R.W. (Ed), *Pathways To Data*, Chicago, Aldine (1970), pp 81-98

Geertz, C., *The Interpretation of Cultures*, London, Hutchinson (1975)

226

Gill, H.S., (a) `Handling redundancies and how to manage morale', *Personnel Management*, Vol.17, No.3, March 1975, pp 34-37

Gill, H.S., (b) `Organisational Behavioural Series - Action Research - A critical examination of its use in organisational improvement', *Industrial and Commercial Training*, Vol.7, No.7, July 1975, pp 286-290

Gill, H.S., *Managing stringency in Higher Education: some issues of organisational design*, Unpublished paper 1981, Department of Management Studies, Sheffield City Polytechnic

Gill, H.S., `Research as action: an experiment in utilising the Social Sciences', *Personnel Review*, Vol.11, No.2, 1982, pp 25-34

Gill, H.S. & Pratt, J., *The Effects of Financial Constraints in Institutions of Higher Education*, Research Report published by The Department of Education and Science, 1986

Ginsberg, S.S., `A comment and elaboration as applied to government and universities' in Cyert, R.M.   (Ed), *The Management of Non-Profit Organisations*, Lexington, Massachusetts, Lexington Books (1975), pp 79-98

Glassberg, A., `Organisational responses to municipal budget decreases', *Public Administration Review*, Vol.38, No.4, July/Aug. 1978, pp 325-332

Glennester, H., `Prime cuts: public expenditure and social service planning in a hostile environment', *Policy and Politics*, Vol.8, No.4, October 1980, pp 367-382

Glennester, H., `From containment to conflict? Social planning in the eighties', *Journal of Social Policy*, Vol.10, No.1, January 1981, pp 31-51

Glidewell, J.C., `The entry problem in consultation', *Journal of Social Issues*, Vol.15, No.2, 1959, pp 51-59

Goffman, E. *The Presentation of Self in Everyday Life*, Harmondsworth, Penguin (1971)

Gold, R.L., `Roles in sociological field observations', *Social Forces*, Vol.36, No.3, March 1958, pp 217-223

Gouldner, A.W., *Patterns of Industrial Bureaucracy*, New York, Glencoe Free Press (1954)

Green, A.C., `Planning for declining enrolments', *School Review*, Vol.82, August 1974, pp 595-600

Greenhalgh, L. and Mckersie, R.B., `Reduction in force: cost effectiveness of alternative strategies' in Levine, C.H. (Ed), *Managing Fiscal Stress: the crisis in the public sector*, New Jersey, Chatham House (1980), pp 313-326

Greenwood, R., Hinings, C.R., Ranson, S. and Walsh, K., `Incremental budgeting and the assumption of growth: the experience of local government' in Wright, M. (Ed), *Public Spending Decisions*, London, George, Allen & Unwin (1980), pp 25-48

The Guardian, London, The Guardian Newspaper Ltd. 25/10/83

The Guardian, London, The Guardian Newspaper Ltd. 26/10/83

Hall, D.T., and Mansfield R., `Organisational and individual responses to external stress', *Administrative Science Quarterly*, Vol.16, No.4, December, 1971, pp 533-547.

Hamblin, A.C., and Adams, P., `Criteria for effectiveness in local government: the position of supervisors in public and private organisations', *Local Government Studies*, Vol.9, No.2, March/April, 1983, pp 21-33

Hamblin, R.L., `Leadership and crisis', *Sociometry*, Vol.21, No.2, June, 1958, pp 322-335

Handy, C., *Understanding Organisations*, Harmondsworth, Penguin (1976)

Handy, C., *Gods of Management*, London, Sovereign Press (1978)

Harvey, J., *Modern Economics*, London, Macmillan Press (1983)

Henley, J.S., *Strategies for Research in Organisations: the case of action research*, Unpublished Ph.D. dissertation, University of London (1975)

Hermann, C.F., `Some consequences of crisis which limit the viability of organisations', *Administrative Science Quarterly*, Vol.8, No.1, March 1963, pp 61-82

Hill, M., `Social work teams and the allocation of resources', in Booth, T.A., (Ed). *Planning for Welfare*, Oxford, Blackwell (1979) pp 115-130

Hills,F.S. and Mahoney, T.A., `University budgets and organisational decision making', *Administrative Science Quarterly*, Vol.23, No.3, September 1978, pp 454-465

Hirschhorn, L. (a), `Managing retrenchment in uncertain times' in Hirschhorn, L. and Associates (Eds), *Cutting Back: retrenchment and redevelopment in human and community services*, San Francisco, Jossey-Bass (1983), pp 15-32

Hirschhorn, L. (b), `Professional team work, autonomous professionals and organisational structure' in Hirschhorn, L. and Associates (Eds), *Cutting Back: retrenchment and redevelopment in human and community services*, San Francisco, Jossey-Bass (1983), pp 109-120

Hirschhorn, L. (c), `Managing resources in retrenchment', *S.A.M. Advanced Management Journal*, Vol.48, No.3, Summer 1983, pp 4-11

Hirschhorn, L. and Associates, (Eds), *Cutting Back: retrenchment and redevelopment in human and community services*, San Francisco, Jossey-Bass (1983)

Hirschman, A.O., *Exit, Voice and Loyalty: responses to decline in firms, organisations and states*, Cambridge, Massachusetts, Harvard University Press (1970)

Holsti, O., `Limitations of cognitive ability in the face of crisis' in Smart, C.F. and Stanbury, W.J. (Eds), *Studies in Crisis Management*, Toronto, Butterworth (1978), pp 39-55

Jaques, E., *The Changing Culture of a Factory*, London, Routledge and Kegan Paul (1951)

Jick, T.D. and Murray, V.V., `The management of hard times: budget cutbacks in public sector organisations', *Organisational Studies* Vol.3, No.2, 1982, pp 141-169

Johnson, J.D., *Doing Field Research*, New York Free Press (1975)

Jones, G.N., *Planned Organisational Change*, London, Routledge and Keegan Paul (1969)

Judge, K., *Rationing Social Services*, London, Heinemann (1978)

Judge, K., `The personal social services', *Local Government Studies*, Vol.7, No.2, March/April 1981, pp 85-90

Kogan, M. with Kogan, D., *The Attack on Higher Education*, London, Kogan Press (1983)

Lawton, W.C., `Sociological research in big business' in Habenstein, R.W. (Ed), *Pathways to data*, Chicago, Aldine (1970), pp 148-162

Levine, C.H., `Organisational decline and cutback management', *Public Administration Review*, Vol.38, No.4, July/Aug. 1978, pp 316-325

Levine, C.H., `More on cutback management: hard questions for hard times', *Public Administration Review*, Vol.39, No.2, March/April 1979, pp 179-183

Levine, C.H., Rubin, I.S. and Wolohojian, G.G., `Resource scarcity and the reform model', *Public Administration Review*, Vol.41, No.6, Nov/Dec. 1981, pp 619-628

Little, R.W., `Field research in military organisations' in Habenstein, R.W. (Ed), *Pathways To Data*, Chicago, Aldine (1970), pp 163-184

Lorsch, J.W. and Lawrence, P.R., *Organisation for product innovation*, Harvard Business Review, Vol.43, Jan/Feb. 1965, pp 109-122

McTighe, J.J., `Management strategies to deal with shrinking resources', *Public Administration Review*, Vol.39, No.1, Jan/Feb. 1979 pp 86-90

Manns, C.L. and March, J.G., `Financial adversity, internal competition and curriculum changes in a university', *Administrative Science Quarterly*, Vol.23, No.4, Dec. 1978

March, J.G. and Cohen, J., *Leadership and Ambiguity*, New York, McGraw Hill (1974)

March, J.G. and Simon, H.A., *Organisations*, New York, John Wiley & Sons (1958)

Martin, R. and Fryer, R.H., `Management and redundancy; an analysis of planned organisational change', *British Journal of Industrial Relations*, Vol.8, No.1, 1970, pp 69-84

Mauksh, H.O., `Studying the hospital' in Habenstein, R.W. (Ed), *Pathways to data*, Chicago, Aldine (1970), pp 185-203

Merry, U. and Allerhand, M.E., *Developing teams and organisations*, Reading, Massachusetts, Addison-Wesley (1977)

Merton, R.K., *Social theory and social structure*, Glencoe, Illinois, The Free Press (1957)

Miller, E.J., `Technology, territory and time', *Human Relations*, Vol.12, No.3, August 1959, pp 243-272

Mitnick, B.M., `Deregulation as a process of organisational reduction', *Public Administration Review*, Vol.38, No.4, July/August 1978, pp 350-357

Murray, V.V. and Jick, T.D., `Taking stock of organisational decline management: some issues and illustrations from an empirical study', *Journal of Management*, Vol.11, No.3, 1985, pp 111-123

Nottenburg, G. and Fedor, D.B., `Scarcity in the environment: organisational perceptions, interpretations and responses', *Organisational Studies*, Vol.4, No.4, 1983, pp 317-337

Ogden, D.M. (Jnr), `Beyond zero-based budgeting', *Public Administration Review*, Vol.38, No.6, Nov/Dec. 1978

Perrow, C., `A framework for the comparative analysis of organisations', *American Sociological Review*, Vol.32, No.2, April 1967, pp 194-208

Perry, J.S. (Jnr), `General systems theory: an enquiry into its social philosophy', *Academy of Management Journal*, Vol.15, No.4, Dec. 1972, pp 495-510

Pettigrew, A.M., `On studying organisational cultures', *Administrative Science Quarterly*, Vol.24, No.4, Dec. 1979, pp 570-581

Pfeffer, J., *Organisational Design*, Arlington Heights, Illinois, A.H.M. Publishing Corporation (1978)

Pfeffer, J. and Leblebici, H., `The effects of competition on some dimensions of organisational structures', *Social Forces*, Vol.52, No.2, Dec. 1973, pp 268-279

Pfeffer, J. and Salancik, G.R., *The External Control of Organisations*, New York, Harper and Row (1978)

Pondy, L.R., `Budgeting and intergroup conflict', *Pittsburg Business Review*, Vol.34, No.3, April 1964, pp 1-3

Pondy, L.R., `Towards a theory of internal resource allocation', in Zald, M.N. (Ed), *Power in Organisations*, Nashville, Vanderbilt University Press (1970), pp 270-311

Potthoff, E.H. (Jnr)., `Pre-planning for budget reductions', *Public Management*, Vol.57, No.3, March 1975, pp 13-14

Pratt, J., `Resource allocation in the public sector', in Morris, A. and Sizer, J. (Eds) *Resources and Higher Education*, Guildford, Society for Research into Higher Education, Guildford University (1982), pp 124-151

Rapoport, R.N., `Three dilemmas in action research', *Human Relations*, Vol.23, No.6, Dec. 1970, pp 499-513

Rose, A.M., `Studying legislators' in Habenstein, R.W. (Ed), *Pathways to Data*, Chicago, Aldine (1970), pp 204-215

Rose, R., `Misperceiving public expenditure: feelings about cuts', in Levine, C.H. and Rubin I. (Eds), *Fiscal Stress and Public Policy*, Beverly Hills, Sage Publications (1980), pp 203-230

Roy, D., `Efficiency and the fix: informal intergroup relations in a piecework machine shop', *American Journal of Sociology*, Vol.60, No.3, November 1955.

Roy, D., `Banana Time: job satisfaction and informal interaction' in Salaman, A. and Thompson, K. (Eds), *People and Organisations*, London, Longman (1973), pp 205-222

Rubin, I., *Financial retrenchment and organisational change: universities under stress*, Unpublished Ph.D. dissertation, University of Chicago (1976)

Rubin, I., `Universities in stress: decision-making under conditions of reduced resources', *Social Science Quarterly*, Vol.58, No.2, September 1977, pp 242-254

Rubin, I., `Retrenchment and flexibility in public organisations', in Levine, C.H. and Rubin, I. (Eds), *Fiscal Stress and Public Policy*, Beverley Hills, Sage Publications (1980), pp 159-178.

Sadler, P.J. and Barry, B.A., *Organisational Development*, London, Longman (1970)

Schatz, M., `Behavioural considerations in management', in Cyert, R.M. (Ed), *The Management of Non-Profit Organisations*, Lexington, Massachusetts, Lexington Books (1975), pp 129-132

Schein, E.G., *Process Consultation*, London, Addison-Wesley (1969)

Schein, E.G., *Organisational Culture and Leadership*, San Francisco, Jossey-Bass (1985)

Schick, A., `Contemporary problems in financial control', *Public Administration Review*, Vol.38, No.6, Nov/Dec. 1978, pp 513-519

Schick, A., `Budgeting adaption to resource scarcity', in Levine, C.H. and Rubin, I. (Eds), *Fiscal Stress and Public Policy*, Beverley Hills, Sage Publications (1980), pp 113-134

Schutz, A., *Collected Papers 1: the problem of social reality*, (Ed) Natamson, M., The Hague, Martinus Nyhoff (1967)

Schutz, A., `The frame of unquestioning constructs' in Douglas, M. (Ed), *Rules and Meanings*, Harmondsworth, Penguin (1973), pp 18-20

Scott, W.G., `Organisational theory: a reassessment', *Academy of Management Journal*, Vol.17, No.2, June 1974, pp 242-254

Scott, W.G., `The management of decline', *The Conference Board Record*, Vol.13, June 1976, pp 56-59

Scott, W.R., `Field Methods in the study of organisations', in March, J.G. (Ed), *Handbook of Organisations*, Chicago, Rand McNally (1965), pp 261-304

Self, P., `Public expenditure and welfare' in Wright, M. (Ed), *Public Spending Decisions*, London, George Allen & Unwin (1980), pp 120-141

Sherif, M. and Sherif, C.W., *Groups in Harmony and Tension*, New York, Harper and Row (1953)

Shibutani, T., `Reference groups and social control', in Rose, A.M. (Ed), *Human Behaviour and Social Processes*, London, Routledge and Kegan Paul (1971), pp 128-147

Silverman, D., *The Theory of Organisations*, London, Heinemann (1970)

Silverzweig, S. and Allen, R.F., `Changing the corporate culture', *Sloan Management Review*, Vol. 17, No.3, Spring 1976, pp 33-49

Sizer, J., *Institutional Performance, Assessment, Adaption and Change*, Paper delivered to the Leverhulme seminar on institutional adaption and change, Bristol Polytechnic, September 1981

Sizer, J., *Institutional Management in Higher Education*, Address to eighth biennial conference of the Organisation for Economic Co-operation and Development, as reported in *The Times Higher Education Supplement*, Times Newspapers Ltd., September 12th 1986, pp 1 and 3

Sofer, C., *The Organisation From Within*, London, Tavistock (1961)

The Standard, London, The Evening Standard Co. Ltd., 25.10.83

Stanley, M., `Nature, culture and scarcity: forward to a theoretical synthesis', *American Sociological Review*, Vol.33, No.6, Dec.1968, pp 855-870

235

Starbuck, W.H., `Organisational growth and Development' in Starbuck, W.H. (Ed) *Organisational Growth and Development*, Harmondsworth, Penguin (1971), pp 11-142

Starbuck, W.H., Greve, A., and Hedberg, B.L.T., `Responding to crisis: theory and experience of European business firms', *Journal of Business Administration*, Vol.9, No.2, Spring 1978, pp 111-137

Staw, B.M., Lance, E.S. and Dutton, J.E., `Threat-rigidity effects in organisational behaviour: a multi-level analysis', *Administrative Science Quarterly*, Vol.26, No.4, December 1981, pp 501-524

Staw, B.M. and Szwajkowski, E., `The scarcity-munificent component of organisational environments and the commission of illegal acts', *Administrative Science Quarterly*, Vol.20, No.3, September 1975, pp 345-354

Stewart, J.D., `From growth to standstill', in Wright, M. (Ed) *Public Spending Decisions*, London, George Allen and Unwin (1980), pp 9-24

Thurley, K.E., `Planning change in bureaucratic organisations', *International Studies of Management and Organisations*, Vol.1, No.3, Fall 1971, pp 253-273

Tichy, N.M., `Problem cycles in organisations and the management of change', in Kimberley, J.R., Miles, R.H. and Associates (Eds), *The Organisational Life Cycle*, San Francisco, Jossey-Bass (1980), pp 162-183

Tills, S., `Understanding the consultant role', *Harvard Business Review*, Vol.39, No.6, Nov/Dec. 1961, pp 87-99

Tolley, G., `Sustained leadership in a situation of zero growth', *Journal of Yorkshire and Humberside Management Centre*, Issue 2 1980, p 7

Trist, E.L., Sushman, G.I. and Brown, G.R., `An experiment in autonomous working in an American underground coalmine', *Human Relations*, Vol.30, No.3, March 1977, pp 201-236

Turner, B., *Exploring the Industrial Sub-Culture*, London, Macmillan (1971)

Turner, V.W., *Schism and Continuity in an African Society*, Manchester, Manchester University Press (1957)

Ullman, J.E., `Nearer my God to thee (or what this needs, Chief, is the hard sell)' in Cyert, R.M. (Ed), *The Management of Non-Profit Organisations*, Lexington, Massachusetts, Lexington Books (1975), pp 141-154

Van der Vall, M., Bolas, C. and Kang, T.S., `Applied social research in industrial organisations: an evaluation of functions, theory and methods', *Journal of Applied Behavioural Science*, Vol.12, No.2, April/May/June 1976, pp 158-177

Warmington, A., `Action research: its methods and implications', *Journal of Applied Systems Analysis*, Vol.7, April 1980, pp 23-39

Warner, K.W. and Havens, E.A., `Goal displacement and the intangibility of organisational goals', *Administrative Science Quarterly*, Vol.12, No.4, December 1968, pp 539-555

Webb, A., `Policy making in social services departments', in Booth, T.A. (Ed), *Planning for Welfare*, Oxford, Basil Blackwell (1979), pp 97-114

Weber, M., *Economy and Society*, New York, Bedminster Press (1968)

Whetton, D.A. (a), `Organisational decline: a neglected topic of organisational science', *Academy of Management Review*, Vol.5, No.4, October 1980, pp 577-588

Whetton, D.A. (b), `Sources, responses and effects of organisational decline' in Kimberley, J.R., Miles, R.H. and Associates (Eds), *The Organisational Life Cycle*, San Francisco, Jossey-Bass (1980), pp 342-374

Whetton, D.A., `Organisational responses to scarcity: exploring obstacles to innovative approaches to retrenchment in education', *Educational Adminstration Quarterly*, Vol.17, No.3, Summer 1981, pp 80-97

Wilburn, R.C. and Worman, M.A., `Overcoming the limits of personnel cutbacks: lessons learned in Pennsylvania', *Public Administration Review*, Vol.40, No.6, Nov/Dec. 1980, pp 609-621

Williams, A. and Anderson, R., *Efficiency in the Social Services*, Oxford, Basil Blackwell (1975)

Wolman, H. with Davies, B., `Local government strategies to cope with fiscal pressures, in Levine, C.H. and Rubin, I., *Fiscal Stress and Public Policy*, Beverly Hills, Sage Publications (1980), pp 231-248

Wood, S., `Management reaction to job redundancy through early retirement', *The Sociological Review*, Vol.28, No.4, November 1980, pp 783-807

Wright, M. (Ed), *Public Spending Decisions: growth and restraint in the 70's*, London, George Allen and Unwin (1980)

Wright, M., `Growth, restraint and rationality' in Wright, M. (Ed), *Public Spending Decisions: growth and restraint in the 70's*, London George Allen and Unwin (1980), pp 142-166

Yarmolinsky, A., `Institutional paralysis', *Daedalus*, Vol.104, Winter 1975, pp 61-67

Zammuto, R.F. and Cameron, K.S., `Environmental decline and organisational response', in Chung, K.H. (Ed), *Proceedings of the Annual Meeting of the Academy of Management*, New York, Academy of Management 1982, pp 250-254